the domaine chandon cookbook

Karen —
Thank you for your
beautiful endorsement
and longtime support.
Lots of love —

Jeff

the domaine chandon cookbook
recipes from *étoile* restaurant

BY JEFF MORGAN
PHOTOGRAPHS BY FRANCE RUFFENACH

CHRONICLE BOOKS

SAN FRANCISCO

Manufactured in China

Designed by Sara Schneider
Food and prop styling by George Dolese
Assistant food styling by Elisabet Der Nederlanden
Typesetting by Janis Reed
The photographer wishes to thank Lara Abbott,
Chef Perry Hoffman, and the kitchen staff at *étoile*; George Dolese
and Elisabet Der Nederlanden; Eric Embry; and Bill LeBlond
and Sara Schneider at Chronicle Books.

10 9 8 7 6 5 4 3 2 1

Chronicle Books LLC
680 Second Street
San Francisco, California 94107
www.chroniclebooks.com

contents

introduction

The year was 1995, and I had just moved to San Francisco to write for a wine magazine. One of my first assignments involved driving north from the city to Napa Valley for a winery event at Domaine Chandon's renowned restaurant. I left San Francisco on a sunny afternoon via the Golden Gate Bridge, cruising along far above the dazzling bay waters.

After a short drive, I could see vineyards and wineries hugging the landscape in a symbiotic embrace. Domaine Chandon's driveway led me on a short tour through the estate and right up to the sleek, modern building that serves as both a winery and a restaurant—the only such establishment in all of Napa Valley.

The scene that awaited me was one I will never forget. In the elegant, airy dining room, with views overlooking the property, it seemed as though every winemaker in the valley had come together for a celebration of wine-country living. Needless to say, sparkling wine flowed, and oysters grown in nearby waters were consumed in profusion. A gala, multicourse meal was soon served, prepared by then-presiding chef Philippe Jeanty and enjoyed by many of the vintners who had made Napa Valley the famous wine region it is today.

What impressed me most was how the culture of the vine and the dinner table were so seamlessly connected. For Europeans, centuries of tradition have made this an unspoken, simple truth. But many Americans have had to discover the marriage of food and wine on their own. For me, Domaine Chandon's event that long-ago day was a testament to a lifestyle forged in Europe yet effectively transplanted—with New World flair—to Northern California.

In this book, I have tried to convey the excitement and the magic that continues to unfold daily at Domaine Chandon both in its restaurant and at the winery. In addition to the recipes, food and wine tips, and beautiful photographs that grace these pages, readers will become intimately acquainted with the estate's history.

Just as I have been touched by my first and many subsequent visits to Domaine Chandon, I hope readers will be inspired by this book to tour the winery and enjoy an excellent meal there. Those who have already had the pleasure of visiting the estate will surely rekindle their memories of fine wine and the seasonal flavors served at the restaurant *étoile*. Here, in the beautiful Napa Valley, the cuisine is paired with top-flight wines to set the stage for the ultimate food-and-wine experience.

Jeff Morgan
Napa Valley

domaine chandon: a french concept takes root in napa valley

In the late 1960s, a visionary group of wine pioneers began to transform Napa Valley into the New World's most renowned modern-day wine region. One of them was a Frenchman named Count Robert-Jean de Vogüé—then chairman of the board at Champagne Moët & Chandon's parent company Moët-Hennessy, in France. The other was an American entrepreneur named John Wright. The two men shared a passion for fine wine, and together they helped shape an American renaissance in wine and fine dining.

At the time, worldwide consumption of sparkling wine was on the rise, but Moët & Chandon had limited production potential from its finite holdings in Champagne, France. In fact, Champagne stocks were dangerously low, and Moët had begun to expand its horizons by making sparkling wine in Argentina.

During a 1968 sales trip to San Francisco, Count de Vogüé serendipitously encountered a group of California winemakers, including the legendary Robert Mondavi, whose wines and enthusiasm for winemaking inspired him to consider a move to California as well. It would take several years for his plan to jell, but the seed had been planted.

At about the same time, international management consultant John Wright had requested a transfer from his New York office to the company's headquarters in San Francisco. He had developed an interest in fine wine while working in Europe and hoped to have more contact with California's fledgling wine industry, an hour's drive north of the city. By 1971, Wright had purchased a small vineyard in Napa Valley, which he worked on in his spare time. He remained a full-time business consultant and researcher.

Not surprisingly, in early 1972, Wright put out a study on the future of wine in America. Needless to say, the report was quite optimistic and accordingly received with much interest by wineries and corporations on both sides of the Atlantic. Moët-Hennessy was among those that took note, and the company invited Wright to visit them in Champagne for further discussion. The meeting led to several others, including a visit by Moët winemakers and executives to Napa Valley.

In Napa Valley, the French discovered a land where more than a century of fine winemaking tradition had previously unfolded with great success. The first Napa Valley grapes were planted by George Yount—not far from where Domaine Chandon lies today—in the late 1830s. By the 1890s, some 20,000 acres/8094 hectares of vineyard were planted, and the region's wines were well known as far away as Paris.

But a combination of factors—including the voracious vine louse, phylloxera, and America's disastrous gamble with Prohibition in the 1920s—conspired to nearly wipe out the local wine industry. By the time Moët's principals came to visit Wright,

Napa Valley remained a fairly open tableau, with a rich wine history but potential that had yet to be fully realized.

The timing couldn't have been better. In October of 1972, Count de Vogüé asked John Wright if he would consider spearheading a project in conjunction with Moët-Hennessy to create a winery dedicated to crafting fine sparkling *méthode traditionnelle* wines in California. After a series of California tastings and more visits by Moët winemakers, it was determined that Napa Valley offered the greatest opportunity. The name, Domaine Chandon, had not yet been determined, but in 1973 the plan became official when Moët-Hennessy announced its project to the general public. John Wright would spend the next four years managing the production of the first wines—with significant assistance from Moët & Chandon's French winemakers—and build the winery that today is tucked serenely into the vine-studded hills of what was once a former cattle pasture. Four years later, the impressive winery and grounds of the first French-owned sparkling wine venture in the United States would be complete.

a sense of place

In the spring of 1973, Wright discovered a 350-acre/142-hectare parcel of land for sale just outside the town of Yountville and at the foot of the Mayacamas Mountains. It was ideally suited to his and his French partners' needs. Eventually, additional vineyard land would be acquired as well, but the winery and its surrounding vineyards would be situated here, just off Route 29 at the gateway to Napa Valley and in a location that offered easy access to visitors.

Plans for planting grapes and building a winery were undertaken, but the immediate needs for crushing grapes in the fall took precedence. With the help of neighboring vintners John and Janet Trefethen, Wright was able to set up a winery within the Trefethen winery to accommodate production until what was to become Domaine Chandon was completed.

A chance encounter led Wright to a meeting with San Francisco architect Bob Mountjoy at Roma Architects, a firm known for its work in national parks. Roma would ultimately design the Domaine Chandon winery. The goal was to create an environmentally sensitive group of buildings that would reflect a contemporary California design aesthetic while also permitting the winery crew to employ time-honored techniques such as those used in Champagne, France. In addition to the winery, plans also called for a visitors' center with a tasting bar and small museum. Ironically, the restaurant did not figure in the original plans.

Construction on the 80,000-square-foot/7432-meter winery began in 1975. Fitted to the curve of the hill, the building was intentionally designed to blend into the landscape. The visitors' center was actually built to accommodate a magnificent old oak that no one could bear to cut down. The great tree is now surrounded by an outdoor terrace where winery and restaurant guests can enjoy an alfresco aperitif and snack. In fact, most of the native oak trees that were growing on the property before it was developed are still there. Rocks from the steep hillsides were also incorporated into the winery walls to create a visual plane with little separation between the natural landscape and the new buildings.

By 1976, three vintages had been produced, but no wine had yet been released, and the winery was still a year from completion. There was still no definitive name for the wine, either. Tentatively referred to as M & H (for Moët-Hennessy), the title did not resonate with John Wright. Finally after much internal debate, Domaine Chandon was selected. The name honored the winery's French parentage as well as its estate concept.

the restaurant at domaine chandon

In January of 1977, winery construction was fast coming to its conclusion. But the visitors' center included a radical design change from the original blueprint. It wasn't until after construction had begun that Wright proposed building a full-service fine dining restaurant on the site. Back in France, Moët-Hennessy had successfully run a private dining establishment for many years. With this in mind, Wright realized that the 1970s Napa Valley restaurant landscape was still in its infancy. He believed a Domaine Chandon restaurant would not only satisfy a need for more top-tier restaurants in the area, but would also encourage visitors to spend more time at the winery.

In Champagne, the principals at Moët-Hennessy agreed with Wright. Unfortunately, local sentiments in Yountville were not so unanimous. Domaine Chandon's first request to Napa County for a restaurant permit was denied. There was simply no precedent for a dining establishment built on land zoned for agriculture. Finally, Wright was able to demonstrate that the restaurant would not compromise the environmental integrity of the property, and the county reversed its decision. (Some old timers insist that the county's motive was linked more to a desire for improved local dining options than to environmental concerns.) Ultimately, the restaurant at Domaine Chandon became a reality—at least on paper—in the first month of 1977.

The original kitchen was built underneath the dining room, which today continues to offer diners a view of the surrounding landscape and neighboring gardens. A team of chefs was brought over from France, including *chef de cuisine* Udo Nechutnys, a protégé of famous French chef Paul Bocuse. Nechutnys was joined by *chef saucier* Philippe Jeanty, who had previously worked at Moët's private dining facility in Epernay, Champagne. Jeanty would become *chef de cuisine* less than two years later, and he remained in charge of the stoves at Domaine Chandon for twenty years before leaving to open his eponymous restaurant, Bistro Jeanty, just across Route 29 in downtown Yountville.

The restaurant opened with quite a bit of fanfare. A combination of white tablecloth dining service and a level of culinary finesse not often seen in the then still sleepy Napa Valley quickly catapulted the restaurant to celebrity status. Within weeks of opening, reservations were hard to come by, and a luncheon buffet was soon embraced by locals and tourists alike. The buffet was replaced by a more traditional menu featuring dishes that were grounded in French tradition but that also reflected the cultural and agricultural influences prevalent in Northern California.

One thing at the now storied restaurant that has evolved considerably since those early days is the wine list. At first, California law prevented the restaurant from selling any wines not produced at the winery. Despite the fact that sparkling wine is a versatile companion for many foods, the law did put a damper on the scope of the offerings from the cellar and the wine service.

To work around the law, Wright encouraged guests to bring their own wine, for which the restaurant charged a small corkage fee—minimal by today's standards. Eventually, the law was amended to permit the restaurant to create an extensive wine list. Over time, the restaurant's wine list has come to represent a diverse cross-section of mostly locally grown wines. With its California focus, the wine list at Domaine Chandon now offers an impressive taste of the best wines from the West, including an unusually deep vertical vintage selection featuring rare old wines.

In a nod to the winery's prestige cuvée, or top-tier wine, in 2006, the restaurant was given the name *étoile*, a word that means "star" in French. Today, *étoile* remains the only winery restaurant in Napa Valley, and both the winery and the restaurant are among the most visited landmarks in the region. In addition to lunch, dinner, wine tastings, and formal tours, visitors can enjoy a leisurely stroll around the property, where they will pass the whimsical stone mushroom garden, the waterfall in the grotto, and the "cascading barrel" restaurant roofline. Eventually, they will walk over the bridge that leads to the restaurant and Visitor Center—a perfect spot to relax on the terrace with a glass of sparkling wine.

Tragically, French founding father Robert-Jean de Vogüé died in the fall of 1976, just a few months shy of seeing his American winery completed. John Wright stayed on to finish the job at hand and steer Domaine Chandon on a steady course. He retired January 1, 1991. The two men, as well as many colleagues who shared their vision, brought Old World tradition and New World ingenuity to a wine region destined to change the drinking and dining habits of a nation.

the tasting bar and the terrace

While the *étoile* restaurant at Domaine Chandon is designed with tasteful elegance, the Tasting Bar and the Terrace are meant for more casual enjoyment. In good weather (which means much of the year in Northern California), floor-to-ceiling windows behind the long tasting counter slide away, blurring the boundaries between indoors and out-doors. For comfort, plush couches add a diverse seating alternative to the long bar and raised tables in the room. Both the Tasting Bar and the Terrace offer guests a long list of refreshing beverages and wine flights as well as a short list of oysters, appetizers, cheeses, and wine-friendly sand-wiches—all perfect for passing a relaxing moment in the Napa Valley countryside.

green farming at domaine chandon

At Domaine Chandon, we have been farming pristine vineyard land in Northern California for nearly four decades, and we strive to be mindful and acutely in tune with the beautiful and both simple and complex physical environment that surrounds us. We understand that only a healthy planet will provide a healthy future for us all.

Sustainable farming practices are the key to this success, and we use a blend of modern science and age-old traditions to cultivate our vines with environmental sensitivity. These sustainable farming practices replenish, control, and often restore natural habitat. We plant nutrient-rich cover crops between the vine rows to nourish our vines and diminish the need for fertilization. These cover crops have the added benefit of providing a home for beneficial insects, such as ladybugs, that help control unwanted insect pests among our vines.

Water also plays an important role in the sustainability equation. While it's obviously an essential agricultural tool, water—through uncontrolled run-off or pooling—can bring about soil erosion or flooding. Domaine Chandon has been commended for restoring anti-erosion catch basins to keep the soil in place and its streams running clear and clean.

Visitors to our vineyards might also notice tactically placed owl boxes built expressly for the indigenous raptor population. The graceful hawks and owls that roost in these cozy nests provide an important and very natural form of pest control.

Creating a small ecological footprint requires thoughtful planning. It's an investment that pays off in our finished wines as well as our future.

the chefs' garden

The *étoile* chefs cook with seasonality in mind, using California fruits and vegetables found in local markets. Our chefs are also blessed with their own full-production, on-site garden and greenhouse. This allows them to cull the freshest of produce for their culinary creations.

In summer, some thirty different vegetables and a selection of a dozen herbs grace the garden and make it possible for the kitchen to incorporate a hefty percentage of its own produce on the menu. From December through March, winter greens, root vegetables, and cold-weather herbs keep the kitchen well supplied. Our greenhouse produces baby lettuces year-round.

Domaine Chandon's chefs farm their own gardens on a daily basis, a tradition that began thirty years ago when pastry chef Francisco Enriquez planted an orange tree, the same tree that today still produces fruit for our signature bitter orange crème brûlée. Working the earth keeps the chefs connected to nature and the ultimate in freshness. It's also the only time of day when they have every excuse for having dirt on their hands.

food and wine pairing:
the basics and beyond

It's hard to imagine a great meal without a great wine to accompany it. At *étoile*, wine-pairing suggestions are indicated on the menu and proposed by our knowledgeable wait staff as well. The extensive California wine list is renowned for a selection drawn from the best producers and vintages in Napa and its neighboring valleys.

At *étoile*, we have a unique synergy that allows chefs and winemakers to collaborate regularly as they fine-tune their respective artistry. Each takes into account the other's creativity when designing and tasting. Our menu is, indeed, conceived with wine in mind; and our wines are made for food.

To make the best decisions about what to drink with your meal, it's helpful to have a general understanding of what makes one wine different from another. And because Domaine Chandon is located in the heart of Napa Valley, we can aptly explore this concept from a California perspective.

California's vineyards produce some one hundred different varieties of grapes—far more than many of us are aware of. Each of these grape varieties can produce a wine "varietal" of distinction. Cabernet Sauvignon, Merlot, Chardonnay, Pinot Noir, and Sauvignon Blanc are among the best known. As discussed in the previous chapter, sparkling wine is often—though not always—made from a varietal blend. Both still and sparkling wines can be made in many diverse styles. Together, they offer wine lovers a broad range of drinking and dining opportunities.

Every wine has a personality of its own, with roots not only in its maker and its genetic makeup, but also in the physical environment in which the grape sources are grown. Cabernet Sauvignon from Napa Valley tends to be richer and more full bodied than leaner Cabernet Sauvignon grown in neighboring Sonoma Valley. The warmer temperatures found in Napa typically cause the grapes there to become riper, which translates to a more full-bodied style. But the cooler temperatures in the Sonoma Valley vineyards give its Cabernets a distinct character of their own, manifested in a light-textured wine with uniquely layered nuances.

Is this good or bad, or just confusing? Actually, it's all quite good. Without variations in style, wine would be boring. No one wants to eat the same food day after day; likewise, we wouldn't want to always drink the same wine. If variety is the spice of life, then California wine is surely a varietal paradise. And exploiting these differences to their best advantage in every vintage is both an art and a science.

making sense of varietals

How do we know what qualities we are looking for in a Cabernet versus a Pinot Noir? Despite regional differences of provenance, California's varietal wines do have certain common traits that help us determine, in a general manner, what we can expect to find in the bottle. The following descriptions highlight some of California's most popular wine varietals.

red wines

Cabernet Sauvignon: Full bodied and richly textured, Cabernet Sauvignon benefits from a broad spectrum of flavors including blackberry, cassis, plum, black cherry, tea, licorice, and even chocolate. It is often blessed with herbal notes, such as thyme and sage, and is generally framed in toasty oak, derived from the barrels used for aging.

Merlot: Similar to Cabernet Sauvignon, Merlot is typically less robust or full bodied on the palate. It serves up comparable fruit flavors to those found in Cabernet, but it often offers softer tannins. As a result, Merlot is sometimes considered to be ready for drinking earlier than Cabernet.

Petite Sirah: This is not Syrah, but instead a distinct grape variety that was created by the French more than a century ago by crossing Syrah with an obscure grape called Peloursin. Petite Sirah didn't go far in France, but it thrived in nineteenth-century California. Old Petite Sirah vines still dot the landscape and can produce wines of exceptional quality. While it may not be widely planted today, it is still enjoyed by many for its deep, dark color and rich, plush, plum, blackberry, and smoke flavors.

Pinot Meunier: A spicier relative of Pinot Noir, this fruity varietal is best known as a blender used for sparkling wine. The word *meunier* means "miller" in French and refers to the floury down on the underside of the grapevines' leaves. Domaine Chandon is the world's leading producer of Pinot Meunier as a still-wine varietal.

Pinot Noir: Pinot Noir is a versatile wine, more light bodied than many other red wines yet blessed with good structure and layers of flavor. At its core, look for pretty cherry notes. They'll be backed by hints of spice, smoke, and herbs. At its best, Pinot Noir is extremely elegant and refined.

Syrah: Occasionally referred to by its Australian moniker, Shiraz, Syrah can be recognized by its earthy overtones and aromas of the forest, like mushrooms and fallen leaves. But California Syrah is also known for its tangy essence of blackberry and black cherry, combined with spicy, herbal notes.

Zinfandel: Sometimes considered a California signature wine because it grows almost nowhere else, Zinfandel is known for its spicy, fruity appeal. The wine is often redolent of strawberries, raspberries, blackberries, and cherries, along with hints of vanilla, cinnamon, and other spices.

white wines

Chardonnay: California's most popular white wine, Chardonnay, takes many forms, ranging from rich and full bodied to lean, light, and mineral-like. Some of this is due to *terroir*, a term that comprises the soil and climate characteristics of the ground the grapes grew in. But the range of styles can also be attributed to winemaking techniques. Toasty Chardonnay that is barrel fermented will taste different from a fruity one fermented in tanks. In general, look among all Chardonnays for an elegant and refreshing wine that shows off pretty apple, pear, and/or citrus flavors. Barrel-fermented versions will be more robust in texture than newly popular "unwooded" Chardonnays.

Rosé: These pink wines have left behind a kind of mid-century misunderstanding as "the other white wine"—meaning to many people, sweet and inelegant—and are experiencing a huge surge in popularity as more and more bottles ranging from delicate to extremely elegant to fun appear on tables, shelves of wine shops, and wine lists. Not long ago, rosé would hardly have been included in a listing of California's most popular varietals. That's partly because rosé is not technically a varietal at all. The word *rosé* comes from the French word for "pink" and simply refers to a wine's color. But today, there is renewed interest in the category that makes it ripe for discussion. Rosé can be made from just about any red grapes, and sometimes white grapes are included in the blend as well. For a winemaker, the trick is to separate the clear grape juice from the red grape skins before the juice takes on a red hue.

Sauvignon Blanc: Best known for its bracing acidity, this lively—almost feisty—varietal is loaded with zippy citrus flavors. Grapefruit and passion fruit often come to mind here as well. Many Sauvignon Blancs are also noteworthy for their distinctively "grassy" aromas that remind us of freshly cut hay. Melon and fig notes can be discerned in very ripe examples of this serious rising star among varietals.

Sparkling wine: As discussed previously, sparkling wine can be made from a single varietal or a blend of white or white and red grapes. The traditional blending varietals in Champagne, France, include Chardonnay, Pinot Noir, and Pinot Meunier. In Germany, Riesling is commonly used to produce excellent sparkling wine. Down under, in Australia, a red sparkling wine made with Syrah—or Shiraz—is quite popular. It's interesting to note that bubbly comes in styles ranging from dry to sweet. For a more detailed discussion, see "A Sparkling Wine Primer," page 34.

other varietals

With limited space, it is fairly impossible to cover the entire diversity of all wine varietals produced throughout California. Other popular varietals to look for include, among reds: Sangiovese, Grenache, and Cabernet Franc (which is related to Cabernet Sauvignon). The white wine varietals Chenin Blanc, Riesling, Gewürztraminer, Pinot Blanc, Pinot Gris (or Grigio), Roussanne, and Viognier are especially worth trying, too. They often show fruit flavors that range from peach to apple and pear, and serve up bright-edged acidity. Riesling and Gewürztraminer can be found in dry or slightly sweet versions—both of which can be tremendously satisfying.

dessert wines

Sometimes referred to as "late harvest" wines, dessert wines retain a significant amount of residual sugar and are almost always, in accordance with their classification, significantly sweet. Any wine varietal can be made in a sweet style, but most commonly, Sauvignon Blanc, Semillon, Riesling, and Gewürztraminer are employed to this end. Red wines such as Zinfandel or Petite Sirah are sometimes made in the robust, full-bodied style found in Port.

a sparkling wine primer

French Champagne and sparkling wine (see page 36 for a discussion of their differences) share stylistic qualities typically described in terms derived from French. Words you often see on the labels of these wines, such as *brut, blanc de blancs,* and *Crémant* can create confusion—even among native French speakers!

The good news is that understanding sparkling wine nomenclature is really not that complicated. Basically, the standardized, descriptive names refer either to the color of the grapes used in making the wine or to the wine's level of sweetness.

Most sparkling wines made in the *méthode traditionnelle* (see page 20) receive a small *dosage* of sugar at the end of the aging process, just prior to receiving their distinctive cork stoppers. This sugar is not necessarily designed to sweeten the wine, but instead balances out the crisp acidity occurring naturally in the grapes. The *dosage* provides structure and elegance in a finished wine.

It's interesting to note that long ago, French Champagne was very sweet. In the early 1800s, a significant amount was sold to purveyors in Great Britain, where the demand arose for bubbly that was less sweet. Over time, Champagne makers began reducing the sugar levels in their wines to a level they called "dry," or *sec* in French. This wine was still quite sweet by today's standards, and eventually a somewhat less sweet version called "extra dry" was produced.

Today, most sparkling wines taste truly dry (not sweet), but the old terminologies persist after nearly two centuries. What's most confusing, of course, is that the descriptive terms for still wines—those without bubbles—are just the opposite. A dry still wine is not a sweet wine. Sometimes tradition makes more sense from a historical perspective than a practical one. As the French might say, *"C'est la vie."*

The term "brut" and others in its category also refer to the level of sweetness or the sugar in a sparkling wine. Brut wines, which by definition contain less than 1.5 percent residual sugar, actually register on the palate as quite dry (as in "not sweet"). *Blanc de blancs* (in English, "white of whites") is a term that refers to the color of the grapes. Sparkling wines with this moniker are traditionally made with all white Chardonnay grapes. *Blanc de noirs* refers to a sparkling wine made with all red grapes (the French call red grapes "black," or *noir*). Most sparkling wines, though, are made from a blend of Chardonnay and red grapes such as Pinot Noir. Sparkling rosé has a pink hue, which more often than not comes from the addition of a small quantity of still Pinot Noir red wine late in the winemaking process.

If it sounds confusing—you're right; it is. At Domaine Chandon, our sweetest sparkling wine is made in an extra-dry style that we call *riche*. To simplify, just remember this: Sparkling wines labeled brut, *blanc de blancs*, or *blanc de noirs* typically taste dry. Anything else—including sparklers labeled "dry" or "extra dry"—indicates a certain measure of discernible sweetness on the palate. Sweeter sparkling wines make fabulous aperitifs or after-dinner drinks. And like their still-wine counterparts, they can also pair beautifully with certain rich, savory foods such as foie gras or spicy dishes.

sparkling wine terms

In light of sparkling wine's diverse array of categories, the following definitions will help readers identify and select the style of wine they prefer. Remember that in these definitions, "dry"—unless otherwise noted—means "not sweet."

Blanc de blancs: A dry, sparkling white wine made exclusively from white grapes, typically Chardonnay.

Blanc de noirs: A dry, sparkling white wine made with only red grapes—typically Pinot Noir and Pinot Meunier.

Brut: A dry, sparkling white wine made from a blend of different white and red grape varietals.

Crémant: A kind of catch-all phrase for many kinds of bubbly—often, but not always, made in a sweeter, creamy, low-pressure style.

Demi-sec: In English, literally "half-dry." Demi-sec wines are quite sweet—in fact, sweeter than those labeled "sec."

Doux: The French word means "sweet," and that says it all.

Extra dry: Sometimes called "off dry," this is a wine that is mildly sweet.

Sec: The English translation means "dry," but a sparkling wine labeled "sec" will be somewhat sweeter than a wine labeled "extra dry."

Sparkling rosé: A pink-hued sparkling wine that generally gets its color from the addition of a small quantity of still red wine. Brut Rosé is the driest version of this pink bubbly, which serves up more hints of red fruit than its white counterparts.

what's in a name? is sparkling wine the same as champagne?

Any wine with bubbles may be accurately called a sparkling wine. Technically, the name *Champagne* is reserved for sparkling wines made in the region of Champagne, France, using methods that conform to the specific wine-making rules of that region. Sparkling wines made in a similar manner from Spain are called *cava*. In Italy, they are often referred to as *spumante*. In the United States, most producers use the general term "sparkling wine" for any bubbly made on American soil.

Nonetheless, some sparkling wine producers outside of Champagne continue to refer to their wines by this name. It's a custom that persists presumably more from habit than anything else. In the early days of California winemaking, it was common to see wines labeled with such unintentionally geographic names as "Bordeaux" and "Burgundy," two other wine-growing regions in France, as well as Champagne. Because of increased sophistication among American wine drinkers, American winemakers have realized that labeling a California wine with the name of a French wine region can be quite confusing for consumers.

Clarity in labeling is a question European winemakers addressed long ago. The 1891 Treaty of Madrid established international trademark and copyright laws that respected grape-growing regions. But the U.S. Senate never ratified the treaty, and these laws were never implemented in America.

Domaine Chandon has always subscribed to the international rules. Respecting our French heritage, we do not use the term "Champagne" to describe our wines—even though they are produced using the traditional winemaking methods from the celebrated French wine region. However, the style of any fine wine is linked specifically to its *terroir*, a French word that describes the natural climate and soil influences affecting grape development in the vineyard. California experiences more sunshine and a warmer growing season than France. As a result, sparkling wines made at Domaine Chandon have distinctive and pleasing differences from those made in Champagne. The Chandon bubblies tend to be more fruit-forward and softer on the finish—a distinction that is cause for celebration. Wines from around the world would be quite boring, indeed, if they all tasted the same.

reserve wines

The concept of a reserve wine has little to do with dryness or sweetness. Traditionally, wineries will blend the best wines of a vintage (or several vintages) to create the ultimate in quality and call it a "reserve." For sparkling wines, after the blend is created, a decision must be made as to how long to age the wine prior to release; the longer the wine is aged at the winery with its lees—natural sediments—still in the bottle, the more complex flavors will develop and deepen (see page 20). Typically, the best, more complex wines will benefit most from extensive lees aging. Aging allows for a more complete evolution of the wines' layers of flavor and structure. Simpler wines have less substance to evolve. They are geared for earlier release and enjoyment.

At Domaine Chandon, *étoile* Brut and *étoile* Rosé are among our top reserve wines. They spend five years on their lees. Our brut-styled Tête de Cuvée—the top of the line—ages for seven years. Chandon Reserve Pinot Noir Brut, Pinot Noir Brut Rosé, and Reserve Chardonnay Brut each spend three years on their lees.

Our nonreserve wines—such as Chandon Brut Classic or Chandon Rosé—are meant to be enjoyed sooner than our reserve wines, but they still must age quietly in our cellar prior to release, spending one to two years on their lees.

the question of vintage dating

Unlike most still wines, which are made from a single vintage harvest, many sparkling wines are created from a blend of several vintages. This practice allows sparkling wine makers to preserve consistency of quality from year to year. In exceptionally good years, winemakers may opt to make a vintage-dated sparkling wine as well. Not surprisingly, vintage-dated bubblies are generally considered to be in the reserve category.

pairing food and wine:
finding the perfect match

Pairing a wine with a particular food or dish is really quite simple. You don't need to be able to describe all of the wine's flavors. Nor do you need to be able to analyze the culinary nature of your meal in great depth. The key to a successful food and wine pairing is being able to define the basic style of food or wine you are consuming.

Style? Isn't that something that refers to the way we dress? In the case of wine and food, style is also a word that means "character"; that is, it comprises the main character traits of what we are eating or drinking. Is a wine full bodied or light bodied? Is it rich and opulent, or lean and austere? Bright, zippy, and fresh? Or lush-textured and round on the palate? Each of these describes a wine's style or personality.

You'll notice we haven't mentioned flavor. Yet much of what is interesting and fun to discover in a wine revolves around its layers of flavor. Nevertheless, in terms of picking a wine for dinner, a more broad-based approach to describing what's in the bottle is more helpful than a litany of descriptors ranging from raspberry, cherry, or cassis to licorice and chocolate. Food and wine pairing is ultimately a question of style first; then comes flavor.

complementary pairings

The easiest way to gauge a wine's suitability for a particular dish is to determine whether the food and the wine share common characteristics. These similar characteristics are often most compatible for pairing. If you can say, "This is a rich dish," then you know an equally rich wine will most likely be in order at the dinner table.

What does it mean to say a "rich" wine? Rich wines—like rich foods—are somewhat weighty on the palate. These richer wines are low in acidity and often higher in alcohol. Most are red wines except—to a lesser degree—certain barrel-fermented white or dessert wines. Rich wines pair well with equally rich meals that might be made with plenty of butter or contain an ample amount of fat—such as what you find in a big juicy steak.

Most white wines have higher natural acidity than red wines. As a result, they tend to be lighter bodied and blessed with bright, citruslike flavors. It's no wonder that white wines pair so well with light-textured fish.

Fortunately, there is a lot of middle ground among the medium-bodied wines and the many foods that are neither rich nor light. Think of poultry or pork, for example. These meats pair quite well with many medium-bodied white and red wines. Pasta, too, can find its wine mate among both red and white wines. To pair a wine with pasta, think about the nature of the pasta sauce—not the pasta itself.

What about sparkling wine? It's interesting to note that many people drink sparkling wine on its own or with appetizers. Its celebratory bubbles, bright texture, and fresh toasty aromas, make sparkling wine a fine foil for starting off any meal or event. But in fact, sparkling wine pairs supremely well with a broad selection of foods. It may be the most versatile of all wines. Highlighted by crisp acidity, bubbly makes a fine match for many seafood dishes and salads. That same acidity also balances the richness found in more full-bodied dishes—from poultry to light meats—providing what is referred to as a contrasting pairing.

contrasting pairings

Exceptions to the so-called rules of food and wine pairing abound. That's part of what makes matching a meal with wine so much fun. Contrasting styles can provide an intriguing balance on the palate. For example, caviar could hardly be described as light textured. It is marvelously rich and blessed with a wonderful briny edge. Yet caviar longs for a refreshing, light-bodied sparkling wine. The wine's bright acidity provides a counterweight to the richness of the caviar. *Vive la difference!*

the perfect match

How do you know what wine to choose for that perfect food and wine match? More often than not, complementary pairings work best. But there is no singular "perfect" pairing required for any dish. Whatever you drink will affect the way you experience your meal, and many options will yield excellent results on your palate. With so many good choices, it's easier than not to make the "right" selection. Ultimately, whatever you enjoy is just fine. Remember that you are your own best arbiter of good taste.

choosing a wineglass

How important is the shape or size of your wineglass? Indeed, the glass we drink from can affect the way we experience a wine. Glass size and shape allow a wine's aromas to collect more or less efficiently as we sniff and sip. When we consider that up to 95 percent of what we taste is really what we smell, aromas do count.

Tradition tells us to serve our red wines in larger glasses than whites. It's a nice custom that helps differentiate contrasting styles. From Europe, we have inherited different glass shapes for different varietals such as Cabernet Sauvignon and Pinot Noir. And the high-walled, narrow flute used for sparkling wine also has its own design logic: The narrowness of the glass slows the speed at which bubbles dissipate. In another sublimely subtle touch, the bottom of the interior of each glass is scored with a small, X-shaped notch to give the bubbles a helpful launch as they travel up the length of the flute. Those same bubbles actively carry aromas to the top of the glass.

The physics of glassware and taste perception could probably fill an entire book. But for most us, one or two styles of wineglasses should easily permit a full appreciation of the artistry that issues from any bottle of fine wine.

Here are some basic points to remember:

Shape matters. Choose a glass with sides that are concave, or tilting inward. This design captures aromas rather than letting them escape too quickly from the glass. The exception to the rule might be the sparkling wine flute. Given the way they respond to effervescence, tall, narrow flutes are quite effective with both inward- and outward-facing sides and lips. However, it's important to note that sparkling wine can also be enjoyed in any fine wineglass.

Size matters. Glassware that is too small will not effectively capture aromas and—ultimately—flavors. As a general rule, a glass that holds 10 to 16 oz/300 to 480 ml is best suited to most drinking options. For home use, the best all-purpose size for fine wine appreciation as well as ease of handling is 12 oz/360 ml. But don't fill these glasses to the brim. Partial pours allow us to swirl our wine and release more aromatics without spilling.

Temperature matters. A wine that is too warm (let's say over 75°F/24°C) will not highlight its best aspects. Holding a glass of wine directly in your palm—and not by the stem—will eventually warm your wine up to your own body temperature, which is far greater than our desired limit.

If you don't have the "correct" glass, don't worry. It's all right to improvise.

sparkling wine at the dinner table

Although it may be known as the ultimate celebratory beverage, sparkling wine often takes a back seat at the dinner table. How many times have you served dinner guests a sparkling aperitif and then shuttled the unfinished bubbly bottle off to the refrigerator when you sit down for the meal?

In truth, sparkling wine is far more versatile at the dinner table than New World tradition would lead us to believe. With naturally bright acidity, sparkling wines such as Chandon Brut and Blanc de Noirs can easily stand up to brightly styled dishes that would overshadow wines with less zip—particularly red wines, typically far lower in acidity than whites.

For instance, salads dressed with vinaigrette are prime candidates for a sparkling wine pairing. If your first course at dinner falls into the salad category, why not continue to drink that sparkling aperitif?

There are many other foods that benefit from an accompanying glass of bubbly. Salty dishes, including smoked fish or cheese, are prime candidates. It's no wonder that briny oysters on the half shell, such as Oysters on the Half Shell with Tarragon Mignonette (page 65), are best with a glass of sparkling wine.

Additionally, spicy foods that might overwhelm a less vivacious wine seem almost custom-made for bubbly. To this end, keep in mind dishes inspired by the culinary traditions of Thailand, India, and Mexico, for example.

Seafood, in all of its light-textured glory, always shines when paired with sparkling wine. Ultra-light Japanese sushi as well as more substantial dishes, such as Coconut Lime Mussels (page 123) or Baked Swordfish with Green Lentils and Ginger Aioli (page 134), will all find a happy match in a glass brimming with bubbles.

Try not to let preconceptions stymie your palate. Sparkling wine easily fits a broad range of dining possibilities, from casual outdoor barbecues to formal dinners. In addition to the previously-mentioned items, poultry and lighter meats—even burgers—can shine in the light of a fine sparkling wine.

sabering sparkling wine

Sabering bottles of sparkling wine is a tradition that dates back to the days of Napoleon, when, it is said, officers on horseback found it easiest to quickly open a bottle of bubbly by slashing off the glass lip below the cork with their sabers. Today, sabering is a ceremony uniquely suited to marking a special event, and one that is performed on occasion at *étoile* upon request (though not on horseback). At the thirtieth anniversary of Domaine Chandon, thirty bottles were sabered at once in a high-flying display rivaled only, perhaps, by Napa Valley's annual Fourth of July fireworks.

At the restaurant, we use a special saber designed specifically to neatly shear off the lip and cork of a bottle. (Don't try this at home.) And, of course, we use our best bubblies—such as our reserve wines or large-format magnums—to honor the festivity. The small amount of wine lost in the sabering is made up for in excitement.

cellaring wines: to age or not to age?

It's true: Good wine can improve with age. But how long do we wait? That's the question wine lovers have been asking themselves since the first wine collector laid down a bottle (more likely a clay amphora) for aging in the cellar.

To be honest, the majority of California's wines drink beautifully upon release. That's because most wineries wait until a wine is ready to drink before releasing it to the marketplace. As a rule of thumb, red wines can take a little longer than whites to mature; by corollary, still white wines typically don't age quite as long as red wines. Non-sparkling rosés are not made for aging and should be drunk sooner rather than later—within a year or so.

It can be argued that wine doesn't necessarily improve with age, but instead simply changes character over time. A wine's youthful, bright, fresh, and fruity qualities are eventually replaced with softer, more subdued, subtle attributes. Not everyone has the same taste, and some people prefer younger, more vivacious wines. Other individuals would rather drink something older—or more evolved. And still others enjoy young as well as older wines. It's easy to appreciate both.

In red wines, a certain astringency that comes from grape tannin will decrease with time in the bottle. The flavors in older red wines change from vivid primary fruits to secondary earth and leather notes. White wines, such as Chardonnay, will lose some of their backbone, or acidity, over time. Their fruitiness will be traded for nutty, honeyed aromas and taste. For both white and red wines, aging yields a softening senescence.

For sparkling wines, the concept of cellaring is not always embraced. Some people are afraid the wines will lose their bubbles (which is true, but it takes many years). Others prefer a fresh, young taste or simply purchase sparkling wine at their local wine shop for immediate consumption. Nevertheless, it's important to note that sparkling wine can age very well, especially when produced at the highest levels of quality and aged in an appropriately temperature-controlled cellar. Back in the late 1990s, Domaine Chandon winemaker emeritus Dawnine Dyer set out to see just how the winery's older sparkling wines were holding up. She went down to the cellar and brought up wines dating from as far back as 1973, the winery's first vintage. These wines had been stored in a cool, moist cellar—perfect aging conditions. Without exception, what emerged from the bottles was a beautiful blend of nutty, honeyed, apricot, and citrus aromas and flavors. The wines still sparkled (albeit with tinier bubbles) and seemed perfectly suited for any special occasion.

It's important to remember that many sparkling wines are blended from several vintages. That's why it's not always possible to know the exact age of a given bubbly. Non-vintage sparkling wines can age very well, but the exact age of the bottle will typically be guesswork. Serious collectors will do best to cellar vintage-designated sparkling wine.

The question remains, "How long?" If you don't have a stable, dedicated environment for storing wines, it's probably not a good idea to collect and age them. But wine is a bit more durable than you might believe, and you can certainly keep bottles at home for several months without difficulty. Remember to keep the wine away from heat or direct sunlight and avoid leaving them in rooms that are warmer than 75°F/24°C or in closets that are located near a furnace or other heater.

If you are considering starting a wine cellar or wine-storage unit, here are some things to remember:

1. Store bottles on their sides to keep the corks wet and prevent them from drying out. (Research has sparked new discussion on horizontal storage for sparkling wines. We have learned that the headspace in any wine bottle is quite humid; in a sparkling wine, the pressure in the headspace results in a constant push of the water molecules into the cork, which prevents it from drying out. So, storing sparkling wine upright may actually be best for longer-term storage. Nonetheless, most collectors continue to store their sparkling wine bottles horizontally without mishap.)

2. Ideally, wine should be stored in a place where temperature shifts are minimal or very gradual—within a range of 50 to 65°F/10 to 18°C.

3. Ideal humidity should range from about 50 to 75 percent (more for wines destined to age beyond 2 or 3 years).

4. If you don't have a cellar, commercial electric wine coolers or storage units offer prime aging conditions for your wines. Try to anticipate your needs, though, as limited space in these portable cellars can fill up quickly.

Under the right conditions, most red wines will age well for at least five to ten years. But many white wines will become tired within this time frame. Exceptions are common, however. For example, sparkling wine and late harvested, sweet white dessert wines have excellent aging potential.

Ultimately, there is only one way to know for sure when a wine has reached its peak. You'll need to taste it. For this reason, it's a good idea to purchase more than one bottle of a particular wine destined for the cellar. With three to six bottles—or even a case—of the same wine, you can monitor maturation and determine when the wine is drinking best. Don't make the mistake of holding on to one "great bottle" for too long. More fine wine has been lost to old age than most collectors would care to admit.

cooking with wine

The Domaine Chandon chefs use wine in many of the dishes prepared at *étoile*. Not surprisingly, many of the recipes in this book also include wine among their ingredients. Wine can be indispensable in marinades and sauces. It's an easy-to-use cooking aid in the pot and the pan, as well as in your glass, for enhancing a meal.

The fruit flavors we experience in a glass of fine wine evaporate on the stovetop. So does most—if not all—of the alcohol that effectively carries those flavors from your glass to your palate. That's why it's not a great idea to cook with expensive wine—the very qualities we seek in the bottle disappear in the pot.

However, the elements that do remain in a cooked wine can be the keys to your success in the kitchen. Wine's natural acidity is its most precious cooking component, adding balance to rich sauces such as the one in Beef Tenderloin with Red Wine Sauce, Truffled Mashed Potatoes, and Haricots Verts (page 162). A wine's acidity also helps tenderize meats like Braised Short Ribs with Creamy Polenta (page 159). Lighter dishes, such as chicken or seafood, may be best prepared with a white wine rather than a red one to achieve the desired color, as with the clear broth in the Coconut Lime Mussels (page 123). And sparkling wine can play an interesting role in cooking as well—for example, the bubbles in Chandon Brut Classic contribute a fluffy, light texture to our Crab Beignets with Ravigote Sauce (page 67).

Avoid cooking with sweet wines, unless you are looking for some sweetness in your food. And stay away from so-called cooking wines, sold in some supermarkets. These typically have been salted to discourage consumption by minors. They will also add unwanted salt to your menu.

If you plan to open a very good wine for a meal, and only a small amount of wine is required for cooking, then it might make sense to use some of the "good stuff" in a dish. But as a rule, it's best to select your cooking wines from your local wine merchant's value selection.

CHAPTER 3
getting started:
sparkling cocktails and appetizers

At Domaine Chandon, simple culinary pleasures create the most festive occasions—especially when paired with a celebratory wine or other form of aperitif. This is most evident at the beginning of a fine meal, when the idea is to whet the appetite without overwhelming the palate. At *étoile* and in our Tasting Bar, we make it possible for guests to enjoy a varied selection of appetizers and drinks designed expressly with this in mind.

In addition to still and sparkling wines, cocktails offer a special touch prior to an evening's prandial pursuits. With its intimate connection to Chandon sparkling wine, the restaurant has developed its own Sparkling Cocktails, a select list of which opens this chapter. These bubbly fruit- and spirit-infused drinks are favored by many regular visitors.

With such salutatory drinks, we may crave a special nibble, and so the second part of this chapter offers a host of our signature small plates to accompany them. Most of the appetizers included here are as simple to prepare as they are to eat, with easy-to-find ingredients that serve to highlight whatever may be in your glass. Truffled Popcorn, airy Gougères, and Crab Beignets with Ravigote Sauce fit this category to perfection. These and several other finger foods can be eaten standing or seated. A few other dishes, such as the Salmon and Tuna Tartare with Golden Whitefish Caviar, are best enjoyed at the dining table, with fork and knife poised. Throughout this chapter, you'll find recipes to make eating and drinking a most pleasurable affair, along with a savvy set of entertaining tips.

recipes

sparkling cocktails

Starting a meal with an appetizing beverage is a tradition shared by both French and American cultures. Today the words *aperitif* and *cocktail* are virtually interchangeable, and a glass of sparkling wine transcends any cultural divide.

At Domaine Chandon, French and American sensibilities have influenced the creative process in the kitchen as well as behind the bar. Blending the best in bubbly with traditional mixed drinks, the restaurant has developed a selection of sparkling cocktails. These are drinks that feature sparkling wine, fruit, juices, spirits, and various aromatic herbs grown on-site at the estate. Some are completely original, and others are redefined classics.

To prepare the featured sparkling cocktails, it is helpful to have a few simple tools at your disposal. A 24-oz/720-ml stainless-steel cocktail shaker makes it easy to quickly chill down a mixed beverage by shaking it vigorously with ice. A cocktail strainer that fits over the shaker will assist in pouring the chilled cocktail. (A fine-mesh sieve will also work to this end.) And a jigger shot measure (½ oz/15 ml and 1 oz/30 ml on opposite sides) facilitates measuring out spirits or other ingredients.

Some of the recipes call for "muddling," a mixology term that simply means to mash or crush. Muddling releases aromas and flavors from various fruits and herbs. Professionals and aficionados at home reach for the tool called a muddler, which is a simple wooden or stainless-steel, flat-ended baton that is employed like a pestle. If you don't have a muddler, use the handle of a long wooden spoon as a substitute.

In terms of glassware, just about anything goes. We suggest a number of options, including sparkling wine flutes (see page 41), tumblers, highballs, rocks glasses, and martini glasses. But you may use whatever glass suits your fancy. (Avoid putting ice cubes in sparkling wine flutes, however. The delicate glass bowls can break easily.)

You'll notice that many of the recipes call for a "simple syrup" to add a little sweetness to the drinks. "Simple" means exactly that: hot water and sugar are all it takes to make this all-purpose cocktail syrup. The easy recipe for Simple Syrup can be found on page 214.

Except when noted, most of these recipes can be made with a Brut-styled sparkling wine or any bubbly that shows little or no obvious sweetness. At the restaurant we often use Chandon Brut Classic or Blancs de Noirs.

A votre santé!

chandon bubble-tini

makes 1 drink

The Bubble-tini is a bit like a bubbly strawberry smoothie. It's best served chilled but "straight up"—without ice—in a long-stemmed martini glass.

3 or 4 fresh strawberries, hulled and diced

½ oz/15 ml Simple Syrup (page 214)

½ oz/15 ml vodka

Ice cubes

1 to 2 oz/30 to 60 ml chilled sparkling rosé

In a cocktail shaker, combine the strawberries, simple syrup, and vodka. Using a muddler or the handle of a long wooden spoon, crush the strawberries. Fill the cocktail shaker about two-thirds full with ice cubes. Cover and shake vigorously for 5 to 10 seconds. Strain through a strainer or fine-mesh sieve into a martini glass. Top with the sparkling wine. Serve at once.

luscious peach sparkler

makes 1 drink

This elegant fruity sparkler is great for summertime, particularly with the freshest of peaches. At the restaurant, we make this drink with Chandon Riche, a sparkling wine made in a very subtly sweet style. On its own, the wine delivers stone-fruit aromas and flavors.

¼ cup/40 g peeled and diced fresh peach

5 to 7 fresh mint leaves, plus 1 small sprig for garnish

½ oz/15 ml Simple Syrup (page 214)

Ice cubes

1 to 2 oz/30 to 60 ml chilled Chandon Riche or Crémant

In a cocktail shaker, combine the peach, mint leaves, and simple syrup. Using a muddler or the handle of a long wooden spoon, crush the peach and mint. Fill the cocktail shaker about two-thirds full with ice cubes. Cover and shake vigorously for 5 to 10 seconds. Strain through a strainer or fine-mesh sieve into a tall highball glass filled with ice. Top with the sparkling wine. Garnish with the mint sprig and serve at once.

chandon pom fizz

A ruby hue makes this festive cocktail (pictured on facing page) particularly attractive. Basically, it's a red sparkler with an orange twist. The pom fizz is best when served in a sparkling wine flute.

½ oz/15 ml Grand Marnier liqueur

½ oz/15 ml fresh or bottled pomegranate juice

2 to 3 oz/60 to 90 ml chilled sparkling wine

Strip of orange peel

Pour the Grand Marnier and pomegranate juice into a sparkling wine flute. Fill the glass to the top with the sparkling wine. Twist the orange peel over, drop it in the glass, and serve at once.

sparkling poire

Poire is the French word for "pear", and this pale gold, fruit-driven drink—served chilled in a sparkling wine flute—has a Continental air of elegance. Although optional, the candied ginger garnish will wake up your taste buds at the outset of an evening's culinary adventure.

¼ cup/40 g peeled and diced Bartlett/Williams' pear

½ oz/15 ml Simple Syrup (page 214)

Ice cubes

2 to 3 oz/60 to 90 ml chilled sparkling wine

1 small piece candied ginger for garnish (optional)

In a cocktail shaker, combine the pear and simple syrup. Using a muddler or the handle of a long wooden spoon, crush the pear. Fill the cocktail shaker about two-thirds full with ice cubes. Cover and shake vigorously for 5 to 10 seconds. Strain through a strainer or fine-mesh sieve into a sparkling wine flute. Top with the sparkling wine. Slide the candied ginger (if using) onto a small wooden skewer and place it in the glass. Serve at once.

chandon brut mojito

The minty mojito is taken to a sparkling new level with this variation on a tropical theme (pictured on facing page). It is *remarkably* refreshing—an excellent opening act for an evening of fun and fine dining.

7 to10 fresh mint leaves, plus 1 leaf for garnish

½ oz/15 ml Simple Syrup (page 214)

Juice of ¼ lime, plus 1 lime wedge for garnish

1 oz/30 ml rum

Ice cubes

1 oz/30 ml chilled sparkling wine

In a cocktail shaker, combine the 7 to 10 mint leaves with the simple syrup and lime juice. Using a muddler or the handle of a long wooden spoon, crush the mint. Add the rum and fill the cocktail shaker about two-thirds full with ice cubes. Cover and shake vigorously for 5 to 10 seconds. Strain through a strainer or fine-mesh sieve into a rocks glass filled with ice. Top with the sparkling wine. Garnish with the reserved mint leaf and wedge of lime. Serve at once.

nouveau riche

Exquisitely easy to prepare, the Nouveau Riche cocktail features Chandon Riche, the winery's off-dry sparkling wine. The wine itself is loaded with pretty fruit flavors and just a hint of sweetness. It hits a high note with the addition of a single, modest ingredient—a twist of lime. For best results, use a long cut of lime peel and twist it over the glass to release the flavorful citrus oils into the wine.

4 oz/120 ml Chandon Riche or Crémant

Ice cubes

Strip of lime peel

Pour the wine into a rocks glass filled about halfway with ice cubes. Twist the lime peel over, drop it in the drink, and serve at once.

how to open a bottle of sparkling wine

Because no corkscrew is required, opening a bottle of sparkling wine requires less technical assistance than opening a cork-sealed still wine. However, the pressure inside a bubbly bottle is a force to be reckoned with. It can be managed effectively in the following way:

1. Remember not to point the bottle at anyone.

2. Always start with a chilled wine. If you don't have one handy, place a bottle in an ice-water bath for 20 to 30 minutes or chill in the refrigerator for 3 hours. (The ideal temperature to enjoy sparkling wine ranges from 45 to 55°F/7 to 13°C.) Your freezer will chill down a bottle within a half hour to 45 minutes. But there's a risk; if you leave the bottle in the freezer for too long, or for some reason forget about it, the wine will expand as it freezes and eventually break the glass. For this reason, chilling in the freezer is not recommended.

3. Towel the bottle dry and remove the foil covering the cork. Chandon bottles have a tear tab for this purpose.

4. Do not remove the wire hood. If you are right-handed, grasp the neck of the bottle with your left hand and place your thumb securely over the top of the cork. Tilt the bottle away from yourself and others, bracing the bottom of the bottle against yourself.

5. With your left thumb still securely over the top of the bottle, use your right hand to loosen the wire hood by unwinding the screw loopwire (about 6 turns counterclockwise) so that it doesn't catch on the lip of the bottle.

6. Firmly grasp the cork and loosened wire with your left hand and slowly twist the tilted bottle—not the cork—with your right hand. The pressure inside the bottle will help you slowly ease the cork from the bottleneck.

7. Continue to keep a firm grip on the cork as you slowly remove it. Try wiggling the cork slightly to allow gas to escape from the sides. The cork should come out with a sigh, not a pop.

savvy entertaining: 10 tips to make your party sparkle

A little advance planning goes a long way in making a party as much fun for the hosts as the guests. The following suggestions will add to everyone's enjoyment.

1. Send out invitations several weeks in advance and remember to follow up with those who have not replied within a week of the event.

2. For larger parties, order any wines that you will need to have shipped to your home 2 to 3 weeks in advance.

3. Check on supplies of glassware, flatware, dishes, and any special cooking equipment that might be required at least 1 week in advance.

4. Put up party decorations and purchase flowers the day before the event.

5. If you are serving mixed drinks, buy enough ice beforehand, as well as ice buckets.

6. Prechill sparkling wines, still white wines, and rosé to somewhere between 45 and 55°F/7 and 13°C. Typically in a home refrigerator that means about 2 hours for best results. If you use ice buckets, count on at least a half hour. (A mixture of half ice and half water is more effective than just ice.) Beware of freezers: If you leave wine inside a freezer for too long, it will freeze, expand, and crack the bottle.

7. Prepare finger-food appetizers or snacks well in advance of your guests' arrival.

8. If you are making dinner, do as much prep work and cooking as you can prior to the party; the idea is to spend more time with your guests at the table than in the kitchen.

9. Experimentation is good—but preferably with the right audience. When trying out a new and possibly challenging recipe, test it in a low-pressure situation with close friends or family first. After a successful test run or two, you'll be able to pull it off with ease for anyone.

10. The cheese course: A selection of cheeses before dessert or in place of dessert offers you and your guests a fine transition to the end of a meal. It's also a perfect pairing to finish off your wine and may even inspire the opening of a new bottle. As we do at *étoile*, try a variety of cheeses—from soft to medium-hard—made from cow, sheep, or goat milk. There is no right or wrong kind of cheese, so whatever you choose will be perfect. Remember to remove the cheese from the refrigerator prior to dinner. It tastes best at room temperature.

appetizers

Aperitifs and cocktails stimulate the appetite as well as conversation or a tranquil moment. With this in mind, it makes sense to have bite-size snacks or small, savory dishes at the ready when enjoying a preprandial drink. The following recipes offer a broad range of easy-to-eat appetizers. Most can be enjoyed without utensils, making them quite practical for enjoyment in a cocktail setting before sitting down to eat. They are relatively simple, yet elegant, and designed to highlight the refreshing flavors found in your glass.

gougères

These fluffy-light cheese puffs are dangerously easy to eat. A perfect finger food for entertaining, they could also be called cheese bubbles, because their interiors are filled with air. Not surprisingly, they pair quite well with their bubble-filled liquid counterpart—sparkling wine. Gruyère cheese, made in the French and Swiss Alps, is a semihard, aged cheese with a nutty quality. In the absence of Gruyère, other semihard cheeses such as Cantal, Asiago, or white Cheddar would make delectable substitutes.

½ cup/115 g unsalted butter

½ tsp salt

1 cup/130 g all-purpose/plain flour

6 large eggs

1½ cups/170 g shredded Gruyère cheese

Preheat the oven to 400°F/200°C/gas 6.

In a medium saucepan over high heat, combine 1 cup/240 ml water, the butter, and the salt. Bring to a boil and stir until the butter has melted. Reduce the heat to low, add the flour to the pan, and stir constantly with a wooden spoon until a smooth dough ball forms and pulls away cleanly from the sides of the pan, about 1 minute.

Transfer the hot dough to a large bowl. Using an electric mixer, add 5 of the eggs, one at a time and beating well between each addition. Continue beating until the eggs are fully incorporated into the dough. Add 1 cup/115 g of the cheese and beat until well combined.

Line two large baking sheets/trays with parchment/baking paper. Using a spoon, place teaspoon-size dollops of dough on the paper, leaving enough space between the puffs for them to double in size.

In a small bowl, beat the remaining egg with 2 tbsp water. Gently brush the cheese puffs with the egg wash. Sprinkle the remaining ½ cup/55 g cheese evenly over the tops.

Bake until the puffs are lightly golden and have doubled in size, 15 to 20 minutes. (If you are using two racks in the oven to accommodate the two baking sheets, switch the top and bottom sheets after 8 to 10 minutes to ensure even cooking.) When the puffs have doubled in size, open the oven door slightly, reduce the heat to 250°F/120°C/gas ½, and continue baking until the puffs are golden brown and appear full of air, 5 to 10 minutes longer. Serve warm or at room temperature.

lemon and herb olives

Visitors to Domaine Chandon's Tasting Bar will discover a selection of tangy, brined olives served along with other wine-friendly appetizers. The olives pair perfectly with any of the winery's diverse sparkling wines. A hint of lemon adds a surprise touch that gives extra lift on the palate. And if you're looking for a bit of heat, add the red pepper flakes. Remember to provide guests with a small bowl for the olive pits.

1 cup/170 g unpitted best-quality cured olives such as Niçoise or Kalamata, or a combination

1 tbsp extra-virgin olive oil

1 tsp chopped lemon zest

¼ tsp dried thyme

¼ tsp red pepper flakes (optional)

In a small bowl, toss all the ingredients together. Serve at room temperature.

spiced pecans

These roasted nuts serve up a fine mix of spice with a touch of sweetness. Whetted by a glass of fresh, cool bubbly, they make an excellent predinner snack. Use them to liven up salads as well (a good candidate is the Belgian Endive with Asian Pear, Spiced Pecans, and Walnut Vinaigrette, page 86). They're also fun to nibble with a sweet after-dinner drink.

2 tbsp unsalted butter	¼ tsp cayenne pepper
1 tbsp maple sugar	Pinch of salt
2 tsp brown sugar/demerara sugar	2 cups/225 g pecan halves
½ tsp ground cinnamon	

Preheat the oven to 325°F/165°C/gas 3.

In a small saucepan, melt the butter over low heat. Stir in the maple sugar, brown sugar/demerara sugar, cinnamon, cayenne, and salt. Add the pecans, stirring to coat well with the butter mixture.

Spread the pecans on a baking sheet/tray and bake until toasty brown, about 15 minutes, stirring every 5 minutes to prevent sticking or burning. Remove from the oven and let cool. Store in an airtight container at room temperature for up to 1 week.

truffled popcorn

To transform mundane popcorn into a chic snack or appetizer, toss it with melted truffle butter and pair it with a flute of chilled bubbly. It's a marvelous match to offer arriving dinner guests. If you're entertaining in a large or meandering space, place several bowls of the popcorn in strategic spots for easy access.

It's crucial to use freshly popped corn here. If you don't own a popcorn machine or have the right pan, the easiest alternative is microwave popcorn. Just make sure to purchase a brand that is marked, "No salt, no oil." And go easy on the salt. Too much of it will diminish the truffled effect. Truffle oil—typically olive oil that has had truffles soaked in it or truffle essence added—is not nearly as expensive as truffles are on their own. Look for a small bottle of truffle oil among the specialty oils at your supermarket. Used judiciously, it will last a long time.

½ cup/85 g unpopped popcorn kernels or 1 bag (2.9 oz/84 g) unsalted, no oil microwave popcorn

3 tbsp unsalted butter

1 tbsp white or black truffle oil

Salt

Put the popcorn kernels in a large, heavy-bottomed saucepan. Place the pan over low heat and cover. Wait until you hear the popping slow down or almost stop. (The popping time will vary depending on your pan and stovetop.) If using microwave popcorn, cook according to instructions on the bag.

While the popcorn is popping, in a small saucepan, melt the butter over medium-low heat. Stir the truffle oil into the butter.

Transfer the cooked popcorn to a large serving bowl or several smaller bowls. Drizzle the truffle butter over the popcorn and toss thoroughly with wooden spoons. Season with salt. Serve at once.

oysters on the half shell

serves 2 to 4

with tarragon mignonette

Less than an hour's drive west from Domaine Chandon lies the beautiful, pristine Tomales Bay, home to a number of the region's renowned oyster farms. One of them—Hog Island Oysters—supplies the restaurant with a steady stream of kumamoto and sweetwater oysters; these are often served on the half shell with mignonette and accompanied by a glass of chilled Chandon sparkling wine.

What is it that makes sparkling wine and oysters such a fine match? The key lies in their contrasting characteristics. Oysters are marked by a distinctive briny, mineral quality that comes in no small part from the seawater the bivalves filter through their plump, rich bodies. The combination of saltiness and richness is balanced by acidity. Like lemon juice and the vinaigrette-relative mignonette sauce, sparkling wine is also blessed with high acidity. It comes from naturally occurring grape acidity as well as carbonic acid derived from the carbon dioxide bubbles in the wine. Bright, bubbly acidity mitigates the oysters' powerful sea flavors while refreshing and readying the palate for another bite-size indulgence.

A plate of raw oysters on the half shell is a classic way to start a meal. While oysters are delicious when dressed with nothing more than a few drops of fresh lemon juice, a mignonette will add a different, more complex set of flavors to the mix. Below, you'll find a version of the restaurant's tarragon mignonette. Have ready small forks for pushing the meat out of the shell and supply plenty of cocktail napkins.

Make sure to purchase raw oysters from a reputable fishmonger, and do not buy oysters that are partially open. Shucking them is not too difficult and shucking knives are readily available for under $10/€7. But if you're not comfortable shucking, ask your fishmonger to do it for you. Nestle the oysters on a bed of crushed ice and eat them within a few hours.

½ cup/120 ml seasoned rice wine vinegar

2 tbsp minced shallot

1 tbsp minced fresh tarragon

Freshly ground pepper

24 to 36 small or medium fresh oysters, shucked

In a medium bowl, combine the vinegar and shallot and let stand for 5 minutes. Whisk in the tarragon and season with pepper. Spoon a little mignonette over each oyster. Serve at once.

crab beignets
with ravigote sauce

makes 15 to 20
beignets;
serves 4 to 8

These fluffy, light-weight beignets—or fritters, as we say in English—make a perfect party snack. Whether piping hot or at room temperature, they are fabulous enjoyed as finger food, dipped in an accompanying *ravigote* sauce. The French-inspired *ravigote* is really a cross between an aioli and a tartar sauce—in this instance freshened up with shallots and fresh chervil. If you can't locate fresh chervil, substitute fresh tarragon.

For the sparkling wine in this recipe, we generally use Chandon Brut Classic, but any dry bubbly will suffice. The wine not destined for the batter will serve as an excellent libation for you and your guests.

1 cup/130 g all-purpose/plain flour

Salt and freshly ground pepper

2 large eggs, at room temperature

¾ cup/180 ml sparkling wine

1 tbsp Dijon mustard

2 tsp red wine vinegar

½ cup/120 ml extra-virgin olive oil

½ cup/120 ml canola oil, plus more for frying

1 tbsp minced shallot

1 tbsp minced fresh chervil

12 oz/340 g fresh Dungeness or other lump crabmeat, picked over for shell fragments and cartilage

In a large bowl, whisk together the flour and ½ tsp salt. Separate one of the eggs and add the yolk to the bowl with the flour mixture; place the white in a medium bowl. Add the sparkling wine to the flour mixture and whisk until well blended and a smooth batter forms. Cover the bowl with plastic wrap/cling film and set aside for 30 minutes to allow the bubbles in the wine to raise the batter (it should rise to about half again its size in bulk).

While the batter is rising, make the *ravigote* sauce. Separate the second egg. Put the white in the bowl with the other egg white and put the yolk in another medium bowl. Add the Dijon mustard and 1 tsp of the vinegar to the yolk and whisk to combine. Slowly whisk in the oils in a fine, steady stream until a thickened and emulsified sauce forms. Whisk in the remaining 1 tsp vinegar and season with salt and pepper. Stir in the shallot and chervil and mix well. Cover and refrigerate until ready to use.

To finish the beignets, pour canola oil into a large, heavy-bottomed sauté pan with tall sides to a depth of 1 to 1½ in/2.5 to 4 cm. Place the pan over medium-high heat and heat until the oil begins to shimmer. While the oil is heating, whisk the egg whites until they form stiff peaks. Using a wooden spoon, gently fold the egg whites into the beignet batter. Fold in the crabmeat gently just until combined.

When the oil is shimmering or showing some small bubbles, lower tablespoon-size dollops of the crab batter into the hot oil (avoid crowding the pan) and fry until puffed and golden brown, 3 to 5 minutes. Use tongs or a slotted spoon to flip the beignets at least once, or several times if necessary, to prevent burning on either side.

When the beignets are done, transfer to paper towels/absorbent papers to drain. Let the oil return to shimmering hot between batches. Serve with *ravigote* dipping sauce on the side.

brandy spiced shrimp

These plump, tasty shrimp/prawns have just enough spice to tickle the palate without overheating it. At Domaine Chandon, we use our own fine brandy, distilled from grapes grown in our vineyards. The small quantity of spirits used in this appetizer serves as a condiment; there is virtually no alcohol remaining in the saucepan after cooking. But the brandy's sweet-edged sherry, caramel, and toast notes remain to offer a refined, subtle sweetness that pairs well with the meaty shellfish.

The red pepper powder that gives these crustaceans kick comes from the southern French town of Espelette, where local farmers air-dry the peppers outside their homes. Look for the paprika-like powder in well-stocked spice racks at specialty-food shops. However, any hot paprika such as New Mexico chile powder will also serve well here.

This appetizer calls for a cool glass of sparkling wine—either a dry-styled Brut or an off-dry sparkler.

2 tbsp extra-virgin olive oil

12 large shrimp/prawns, peeled and deveined

3 tbsp brandy

1 tbsp unsalted butter

½ tsp salt

1 tsp *piment d'Espelette* or other hot paprika or red chile powder

Fresh basil, for garnish (optional)

In a medium saucepan, heat the olive oil over medium-high heat. When the oil starts to shimmer, add the shrimp/prawns and sauté until they begin to turn pink, 30 to 45 seconds. Using tongs or a slotted spoon, turn the shellfish and sauté for 30 to 45 seconds longer.

Add the brandy and cook, stirring frequently, until slightly reduced, about 1 minute. Add the butter to the pan and let it melt into the brandy. Stir to coat the shrimp/prawns evenly with the sauce. Sprinkle with the salt and *piment d'Espelette* and stir to mix well. Taste and adjust the seasoning.

Transfer to a serving platter and garnish, if desired. Serve at once.

salmon and tuna tartare
with golden whitefish caviar

American golden whitefish caviar is a light-colored and mild—and more affordable—version of the much-loved delicacy made from sturgeon eggs. It also has more crunch than the traditional black caviars. This presentation features multicolored layers of flavor in a neat, round, savory cake. To give this pretty presentation its shape, you will need a set of four pastry ring molds, available in any kitchen-goods store or online. In specialty-food stores, you can find golden whitefish caviar infused with natural flavorings such as ginger or truffle, either of which would be fun to try here.

In your glass, a chilled, dry sparkling wine is the perfect complement.

Juice of 1 lime	2 oz/55 g sushi-grade salmon, finely diced
1 tsp extra-virgin olive oil	2 oz/55 g sushi-grade tuna, finely diced
1 tbsp minced fresh cilantro/fresh coriander	4 oz/115 g golden whitefish caviar
½ tsp seeded and minced jalapeño chile	4 tsp crème fraîche
1 tbsp pine nuts, toasted (see page 212)	Lime zest, for garnish
Coarse salt and freshly ground pepper	Toast points for serving (optional)

In a small bowl, combine the lime juice, olive oil, cilantro/fresh coriander, jalapeño, and pine nuts. Stir to mix well and season with salt and pepper. Place the salmon and tuna in separate small bowls. Divide the lime juice mixture evenly between the bowls of fish. Stir gently to mix.

Place a 3-in/7.5-cm ring mold with 2-in/5-cm sides on each of 4 salad plates. Divide the salmon mixture evenly among the molds and pat it down into a smooth, even layer. Repeat the process to make a second layer with the tuna. Using about two-thirds of the caviar total for the 4 molds, create a third layer on top of the tuna, patting gently to smooth the surface. Dollop 1 tsp of the crème fraîche on top of each salad. Refrigerate until set and chilled, at least 20 minutes or up to 1 hour. Remove from the refrigerator and gently lift off the molds. (They should come off easily.) Garnish each serving with a dollop of the remaining caviar or lime zest, dividing it evenly. Serve at once, "straight up" with a knife and fork or with the toast points (if using) for spreading.

deviled quail eggs
with caviar

makes 40
appetizers

This hors d'oeuvre is an eye-catching display of black caviar set on a miniature bed of onion-laced deviled egg. Each tiny quail egg sits snugly on a little round brioche toast and requires only a pinch of caviar to complete the picture. They are easy to serve to dinner guests upon arrival or to a circulating cocktail crowd, and may serve to prompt some lively discussion, too. Popping a little egg into your mouth and washing it down with a glass of chilled sparkling wine makes a stunning equation on the palate.

You can find quail eggs in specialty-food shops. Peeling and preparing them is a task geared toward cooks with a gentle touch.

1 loaf brioche bread, cut into slices ¼ in/6 mm thick

2 tbsp minced shallot

1 tsp fresh lemon juice

20 quail eggs

2 tbsp crème fraîche

1 tsp Dijon mustard

Salt and freshly ground pepper

1 oz/30 g imported or domestic caviar

4 or 5 fresh chives, snipped into pieces about ½ in/12 mm long

Preheat the oven to 350°F/180°C/gas 4.

Using a 2-in/5-cm round cookie cutter or the rim of a narrow glass (such as a Champagne flute) of about that size in diameter, cut out rounds of bread from the brioche slices, avoiding the crusts. (You should be able to cut 2 or 3 rounds from each slice.) Using your finger and thumb, pinch a small indentation about ½ in/12 mm in diameter into the center of each brioche round (these will hold the quail eggs). Place the rounds on a baking sheet/tray and bake until golden brown, 10 to 12 minutes. Remove from the oven and set aside.

In a medium bowl, toss together the shallot and lemon juice. Set aside.

Place the quail eggs in a medium saucepan and add cold water to cover by 2 in/5 cm. Bring to a boil over high heat, then reduce the heat to medium-low and cook the eggs for 3 minutes to hard-boil. Remove from the heat, carefully pour off the hot water, and rinse the eggs with cold tap water. Let the eggs stand in cold water for 5 minutes.

Carefully crack the eggs and peel away their shells, starting at the wide bottom end of each egg. Once peeled, rinse each egg with cold water to remove any remaining small bits of shell. Set the eggs on paper towels/absorbent papers to dry. Using a sharp paring knife, cut each egg in half lengthwise. Remove the yolks with the tip of the paring knife or a very small spoon and place them in the bowl with the shallot and lemon juice mixture. Set the empty egg-white halves aside.

CONTINUED

Add the crème fraîche, mustard, and salt and pepper to taste to the yolks. Using a fork, mash the yolks until a thick paste forms and all the ingredients are well combined.

Using a very small spoon or the tip of a dinner knife, fill the cavity of each egg-white half with the yolk mixture. If necessary, gently tamp the mixture down with your thumb. Set each filled egg half in the cavity of a toasted brioche round.

Place a tiny dollop of caviar on top of each egg. Garnish each with a chive piece. If not serving immediately, cover with plastic wrap/cling film and refrigerate for up to 8 hours. Serve chilled or at room temperature.

french onion tart

makes 30 to 40
2- to 3-in/
5- to 7.5-cm
square tartlets;
or serves 8 as
a first course

Depending on how you slice it, this popular tart from southern France can serve as bite-size hors d'oeuvres or a first course to be eaten with a fork and knife. Sweet, caramelized onions are the main attraction here, and they pair beautifully with a glass of toasty, fresh bubbly. To serve as a first course, cut each tart into four individual servings. Enjoy warm or at room temperature.

The dough is not hard to make but requires 2 hours' rising time. An easy alternative is to purchase commercial pizza dough (enough for two pies) at your local grocery store or pizzeria.

FOR THE DOUGH:

1 envelope (2½ tsp) active dry yeast

1¼ cups/300 ml warm water

½ cup/65 g high-gluten flour

2 cups/255 g unbleached all-purpose/plain flour, plus more for kneading and rolling

2 tbsp extra-virgin olive oil, plus more for greasing

½ tsp salt

FOR THE TOPPING:

¼ cup/60 ml extra-virgin olive oil, plus 2 tsp (if needed)

6 garlic cloves, minced

5 tsp dried thyme

6 large yellow onions, halved and thinly sliced crosswise

1½ tsp salt

½ tsp freshly ground pepper

30 to 40 small Niçoise or Kalamata olives, pitted and halved

Fresh thyme leaves for garnish (optional)

TO MAKE THE DOUGH: In a large bowl, add the yeast to 1 cup/240 ml of the warm water. Using a wooden spoon, stir in the high-gluten flour. Add the all-purpose/plain flour, 2 tbsp olive oil, and salt. Stir until a sticky dough begins to form on the bottom of the bowl. Add the remaining ¼ cup/60 ml warm water and stir to combine. Using your hands, shape the dough into a large ball.

Knead the dough in the bowl, pushing it down with the heel of your hand, then pulling it together in a mound. As your hands become too sticky to work, dust them with a little all-purpose/plain flour. Continue kneading until the dough becomes firm yet elastic, about 5 minutes.

Lightly oil a clean large bowl. Transfer the dough to the oiled bowl and turn to coat. Cover the bowl with plastic wrap/cling film and set aside. Let rise at room temperature until doubled in size, about 2 hours.

When the dough has risen, turn it out onto a lightly floured work surface and cut it in half. (If not using the dough immediately, place each half in a separate lightly oiled bowl. Cover the bowls with plastic wrap/cling film and refrigerate for up to 8 hours. Be sure to let them come to room temperature before rolling out.)

CONTINUED

TO MAKE THE TOPPING: In a large frying pan or sauté pan, heat the ¼ cup/60 ml olive oil over medium heat. Add the garlic and dried thyme and sauté for 30 seconds. Add the onions, separating the slices with a wooden spoon and stirring to coat them evenly with the oil, garlic, and thyme. Add the salt and pepper and stir to coat well. Reduce the heat to low and simmer, stirring every 5 minutes, until the onions are quite soft, about 20 minutes.

While the onions are cooking, preheat the oven to 500°F/260°C/gas 10. Have ready two nonstick 9 by 13-in/23-by-33-cm baking sheets/trays or two round baking sheets/trays 12 to 14 in/30 to 35.5 cm in diameter. (If you don't have nonstick pans, lightly oil each pan with 1 tsp olive oil.)

Meanwhile, on the lightly floured work surface, using a rolling pin, flatten each dough piece to fit your pans. Place the dough on the pans and use your fingertips to nudge it into the edges and corners. Raise the outer edge with your thumbs to make a rim.

Spread the topping evenly over the tarts, dividing it evenly. Dot the tarts with the olives. Bake until the edges of the crust are golden brown, 12 to 15 minutes. Transfer to a cutting board and let cool slightly. Garnish with the fresh thyme, if desired.

Cut each tart into 2- to 3-in/5- to 7.5-cm squares and arrange the hors d'oeuvres on a large serving platter, or cut each tart into fourths for individual servings. Serve warm or at room temperature.

parmesan soufflé
with puréed leek

This feather-light soufflé is loaded with toasty Parmesan flavors and subtle garlic notes. The leek topping adds a refreshing herbal touch as well as visual contrast. As with most soufflés, serve soon after it comes out of the oven. If you wait too long, the dramatic puffiness will deflate and the top will sink. Sparkling wine, Sauvignon Blanc, or a crisp, steely, unoaked Chardonnay are excellent wine pairings with this recipe, an equally fine candidate for an appetizer or brunch.

FOR THE PURÉED LEEK:

1 tbsp unsalted butter

1 leek, white and tender green parts, cut into rounds ½ in/12 mm thick and rinsed and drained thoroughly

1 cup/240 ml Chicken Stock (page 216) or canned low-sodium chicken broth

Salt and freshly ground pepper

FOR THE SOUFFLÉ:

5 tbsp/70 g unsalted butter

5 tbsp/40 g all-purpose/plain flour

10 garlic cloves, peeled but left whole

1 cup/240 ml whole milk

1 cup/115 g grated Parmesan cheese

4 large eggs, separated

¼ tsp salt

Freshly ground pepper

TO MAKE THE PURÉED LEEK: In a medium saucepan, melt the butter over medium heat. Add the leek and stir to coat with the butter. Add the stock and salt and pepper to taste and bring to a boil over high heat. Reduce the heat to low and simmer until the leek is tender, 10 to 12 minutes. Transfer the leek and its cooking liquid to a food processor or blender and process to a smooth purée. Taste and adjust the seasoning. Set aside.

TO MAKE THE SOUFFLÉ: Position a rack in the upper third of the oven and preheat to 425°F/ 220°C/gas 7. Coat six 6-oz/170-g ramekins with 2 tbsp of the butter and dust them with 2 tbsp of the flour. Turn the ramekins upside down and tap them gently to remove any loose or excess flour.

Put the garlic in a small saucepan and add cold water to cover. Bring to a boil over high heat, then reduce the heat to medium-low and simmer until the garlic is soft, 6 to 8 minutes. Drain in a colander and rinse under cold running water. Crush the garlic through a garlic press or put them in a small bowl and mash them with a fork. Set aside.

In a medium saucepan over medium-low heat, melt the remaining 3 tbsp butter. Whisk in the remaining 3 tbsp flour. Using a wooden spoon, stir the mixture occasionally until it becomes golden and smells nutty, about 3 minutes. Add the milk and whisk until well incorporated. Raise the heat to medium-high and bring to a boil. As soon as the mixture reaches a boil, remove the pan from the heat and let cool to room temperature, 10 to 15 minutes. Add the cheese, egg yolks, crushed garlic, salt, and pepper to taste and, using the wooden spoon, stir until well combined. Set aside.

In a large bowl, using an electric mixer, beat the egg whites until stiff peaks form. Fold half of the egg whites into the cheese mixture to lighten it, then fold in the remaining egg whites just until no white streaks remain.

Ladle or spoon the soufflé batter into the prepared ramekins, filling them about three-fourths full. Arrange the ramekins on a baking sheet/tray and place on the upper rack in the oven. Bake until the soufflés rise to the top or just over the top of each ramekin and turn golden brown, 10 to 15 minutes. While the soufflés are baking, reheat the leek purée over low heat.

When the soufflés are done, remove them from the oven and spoon a dollop of puréed leek over the top of each. Serve at once.

CHAPTER 4
salads and soups

In a sense, soups and salads are the most versatile of dishes. They can serve as an introduction to a multicourse meal, or they can be the centerpiece of a snack, a light lunch, or an elegant dinner.

Some salads, such as the Belgian Endive with Asian Pear, Spiced Pecans, and Walnut Vinaigrette, might best whet the palate at the beginning of an enticing meal. Other salads with a bit more substance, such as the Ahi Tuna Salade Niçoise, feature well as an impressive main course. In a similar vein, you might find the Green Vegetable Gazpacho with Tiger Shrimp and Pickled Red Onions an excellent choice for a refreshing summertime lunch. In fall and winter, Sugar Pie Pumpkin Soup with Glazed Chestnuts can fill the same niche. By contrast, Sunchoke Soup with Shiitake Mushrooms and Crème Fraîche is less filling and better suited to being an opening attraction.

Soups and salads get high marks for an endless range of flavors and textures, as well as a satisfying sense of healthful indulgence. Pair them with crusty, country breads or enjoy one followed by the other. Both are eminently wine-friendly. Remember that salads—generally dressed in a tangy vinaigrette—are best enjoyed in the company of equally bright-edged wine varietals that offer good acidity, such as sparkling or certain still white wines. Soups, on the other hand, can be rich and full-bodied or light and lively. As a result, wine pairing suggestions for the liquid recipes in this chapter may be more varied than those suggested with the salads.

recipes

carrot and hearts of palm salad

with kumquats, cumin seeds, and tangerine-curry vinaigrette

A riotous mingling of flavors bursts forth from this colorful salad. Toasted cumin seeds, tangy kumquats, and cilantro give simple carrots and hearts of palm a fresh new personality, fashionably dressed in a curry vinaigrette with a tangerine twist. The *étoile* chefs like to use purple carrots (as shown in the photograph) from the Domaine Chandon garden when available. But any carrot—including the common orange variety—will make this salad sublime. To create "ribbons" of carrot and hearts of palm, use a vegetable peeler and shave very thin slices.

White wines with citrusy notes, such as sparkling wine or Sauvignon Blanc, will pair well here.

1 tbsp cumin seeds

10 medium carrots, peeled and cut into thin strips or ribbons about 2 in/5 cm long (about 4 cups/570 g)

1 can (14 oz/400 g) hearts of palm, rinsed, drained, and cut into thin strips or ribbons about 2 in/5 cm long

6 kumquats, halved lengthwise, seeded, and cut crosswise into thin slices

3 tbsp finely diced red onion

⅓ cup/10 g minced fresh cilantro/ fresh coriander, plus sprigs for garnish

3 tbsp extra-virgin olive oil

¼ cup/60 ml fresh tangerine juice or orange juice

1 tbsp white wine vinegar

1 tbsp Dijon mustard

1 tsp curry powder

Salt and freshly ground pepper

In a small frying pan over medium heat, toast the cumin seeds, stirring frequently, until fragrant, 3 to 4 minutes. Transfer to a plate and set aside.

In a large bowl, combine the carrots, hearts of palm, kumquats, red onion, minced cilantro/ fresh coriander, and cumin seeds. Toss gently to mix.

In a small bowl, whisk together the olive oil, tangerine juice, vinegar, mustard, and curry powder until the dressing thickens and all the ingredients are thoroughly blended.

Pour the dressing over the carrot mixture and toss thoroughly to coat evenly. Season with salt and pepper. Divide among salad plates, garnish with the cilantro sprigs, and serve at once.

serves 4

belgian endive
with asian pear, spiced pecans, and walnut vinaigrette

This is a refreshingly different salad that holds myriad flavors in its bowl. Asian pear and fennel lend a slightly exotic note, highlighted by crunchy Spiced Pecans. If you can't find the firm, mild Asian pear, substitute a Bosc pear. Make the pecans in advance; they require 15 minutes in the oven and about the same amount of time to cool down. You'll have extra nuts, which you can use for snacks or to serve guests as a simple appetizer on their own.

Showing just a hint of sweetness, this first course would pair easily with an off-dry sparkling wine such as Chandon's own Riche. Fruity still wines like Riesling and Gewürztraminer match well here, too.

2 tbsp toasted walnut oil

1 tbsp extra-virgin olive oil

1 tbsp Champagne vinegar or white wine vinegar

1 tsp Dijon mustard

1 shallot, minced

1 garlic clove, minced

Leaves from 3 Belgian endives/chicories

1 head frisée lettuce, cored and coarsely chopped

1 fennel bulb, core and stalks removed, sliced paper-thin

1 Asian pear, cored and cut into matchsticks about ¼ in/6 mm thick

Salt and freshly ground pepper (optional)

⅓ cup/40 g Spiced Pecans (page 63)

20 leaves fresh tarragon

In a large salad bowl, combine the walnut oil, olive oil, vinegar, mustard, shallot, and garlic. Stir until the vinaigrette thickens and all the ingredients are thoroughly blended.

Add the endives/chicories, frisée, fennel, and pear to the bowl. Toss gently until evenly coated with the vinaigrette. Season with salt and pepper, if desired. Divide among 4 salad plates and garnish with the pecans and fresh tarragon. Serve at once.

savory bread salad
with baby lettuce, boquerones, and preserved lemon

This fresh green salad serves up an especially interesting blend of flavors and textures. Homemade croutons offer a pleasing crunch. And the silvery, briny *boquerones*—a pickled Spanish anchovy fillet that bears no resemblance to the ubiquitous canned version—marry beautifully with anise-flavored fresh chervil. (Use fresh tarragon if you can't find chervil.) *Boquerones* can be found in most specialty-food stores. Tangy preserved lemons, which have been pickled in salt and their own juices, are easy to make at home, but it takes at least 3 weeks for the lemons to be ready to use. Excellent preserved lemons are readily available purchased in gourmet and Middle Eastern food shops.

¼ cup/60 ml extra-virgin olive oil, plus 3 tbsp

3 garlic cloves, minced

Salt

3 cups/345 g diced baguette or country bread (½-in/12-mm cubes, with crust intact)

1 tbsp fresh lemon juice

½ tsp dried thyme

3 thin slices red onion, cut in half

½ cup/15 g coarsely chopped fresh basil

¼ cup/7 g coarsely chopped fresh chervil or tarragon

12 *boquerones*, drained and halved

2 tbsp minced preserved lemon rind

½ cup/70 g pitted Kalamata olives, halved

12 cherry tomatoes, halved

6 to 8 oz/170 to 225 g mixed baby lettuce leaves (about 3 cups)

Freshly ground pepper

Preheat the oven to 325°F/165°C/gas 3.

In a large bowl, combine the ¼ cup/60 ml olive oil with two-thirds of the minced garlic and a pinch of salt and stir to mix. Add the bread cubes to the bowl and toss to coat evenly with the seasoned oil. Spread the bread cubes out on a large baking sheet/tray and toast in the oven until lightly browned, about 20 minutes. The croutons should be crisp and toasty. Remove from the oven and let cool to room temperature.

While the croutons are toasting, in a large salad bowl, combine the 3 tbsp olive oil, the lemon juice, the remaining minced garlic, the thyme, and the onion. Stir to mix well. Taste and adjust the seasoning. Let stand at room temperature for at least 15 minutes and up to 1 hour.

Immediately before serving, add the basil, chervil, *boquerones*, preserved lemon, olives, tomatoes, and lettuce to the bowl with the dressing and toss well. Add the croutons and toss again. Taste and adjust the seasoning with salt and pepper. Divide among salad plates and serve at once.

warm wild mushroom salad

Earthy mushrooms take center stage in this fragrant appetizer. They offer a panoply of forest flavors. If you can't find wild mushrooms to suit your taste, use a combination of white button or cremini/brown mushrooms and shiitakes.

Wine possibilities are legion here. A buttery Chardonnay or a spicy Gewürztraminer would be excellent. Pinot Noir or gamey Syrah are equally stellar choices among reds.

5 tbsp/75 ml extra-virgin olive oil

½ cup/85 g diced pancetta

1 shallot, thinly sliced

2 garlic cloves, minced

1 lb/455 g mixed wild mushrooms, brushed clean and sliced

1 tsp dried thyme

8 slices ciabatta or other crusty fresh bread

2 cups/115 g chopped red chard

1 tbsp balsamic vinegar

Salt and freshly ground pepper

Preheat the oven to 350°F/180°C/gas 4.

In a large sauté pan or frying pan, heat 2 tbsp of the olive oil over medium-high heat. Add the pancetta and sauté until golden brown, about 3 minutes. Reduce the heat to medium, add the shallot and garlic, and sauté until fragrant, about 45 seconds. Add the mushrooms and thyme. Stir to mix well and cook, stirring occasionally, until the mushrooms have wilted and released most of their liquid, 5 to 7 minutes.

Meanwhile, brush the bread slices on both sides with the remaining 3 tbsp olive oil. Place the slices on a baking sheet/tray and toast in the oven until golden, about 10 minutes.

Stir the chard into the mushroom mixture and sauté until the chard is tender, about 3 minutes. Add the vinegar to the pan and stir to mix thoroughly. Remove from the heat. Season with salt and pepper.

Divide the warm mushroom salad among salad plates. Serve at once with the warm toasts on the side.

ahi tuna salade niçoise

In the southern French city of Nice, the eponymous *salade Niçoise* is served widely and with many variations. Locals are hard-pressed to agree on any definitive version, but key ingredients typically include potatoes, string beans, hard-boiled eggs, tomatoes, olives, and tuna—the latter usually precooked and marinated in olive oil.

This version uses fresh ahi tuna, seared medium-rare. Although refreshingly light on a warm summer afternoon, *salade Niçoise* is fairly substantial and easily serves as a main course for a light lunch. In Nice it is often enjoyed accompanied by a glass of chilled dry rosé. Of course, a sparkling rosé would be an excellent pairing choice as well, as would most bright-textured still and sparkling white wines.

You can boil the eggs in advance and store them in the refrigerator, in their shells, for up to 24 hours.

4 large eggs

1½ lb/680 g new white potatoes, quartered

1 lb/455 g haricots vert, trimmed and cut into 4-in/10-cm lengths

Salt

1 lb/455 g sushi-grade ahi tuna steaks

4 tbsp/60 ml extra-virgin olive oil, plus more for drizzling

1 tbsp balsamic vinegar or red wine vinegar

1 tsp Dijon mustard

1 tsp dried thyme

4 oz/115 g mixed baby greens such as spinach, arugula/rocket, and spring lettuces

½ red onion, thinly sliced

¼ cup/35 g Niçoise or other small black olives, with pits

8 to 10 cherry tomatoes (about 1 cup/170 g), halved

Freshly ground pepper

Put the eggs in a medium saucepan and add cold water to cover. Bring to a boil over high heat, then reduce the heat to medium-low and simmer for 10 minutes. Drain and rinse under cold running water until the eggs are cool enough to handle. Crack each egg at the wide end, where you may find an air pocket, and peel. Put the peeled eggs in a bowl and refrigerate until ready to serve.

Put the potatoes in a large pot and add cold water to cover by 2 in/5 cm. Bring to a boil over high heat. Reduce the heat to medium and cook for 8 minutes. Add the string beans to the pot, cover, and cook until the potatoes are tender enough to be easily pierced with a fork and the string beans are tender but still firm, about 3 minutes longer. Drain in a colander and immediately rinse under cold water to halt the cooking. Set aside the potatoes and string beans to drain completely.

Lightly salt the tuna steaks on both sides. In a medium sauté pan or frying pan, heat 1 tbsp of the olive oil over medium-high heat until the pan is quite hot, about 2 minutes. Add the tuna steaks to the pan and sear until they start to flake, about 3 minutes per side. (For very rare tuna, sear for 2 minutes per side.) Transfer the steaks to a carving board and let rest. When cool enough to handle, cut the steaks into slices ¼ in/6 mm thick and set aside.

In a large salad bowl, combine the remaining 3 tbsp olive oil, the vinegar, mustard, thyme, and a pinch of salt. Using a wooden spoon, stir until the vinaigrette thickens and all the ingredients are thoroughly blended. Add the baby greens, potatoes, string beans, onion, and olives to the bowl and toss to coat all the ingredients thoroughly with the vinaigrette.

Divide the vegetables among 4 large salad plates. Cut the hard-boiled eggs into 4 wedges. Alternate the egg and tomato halves in a circular pattern on top of the vegetables. Lay 3 or 4 slices of tuna over the eggs and tomatoes, and drizzle each salad lightly with olive oil. Season with additional salt and pepper and serve at once.

crab salad
with fennel, rhubarb, and madeira gelée

serves 6
as a first course,
4 as a main
course

This refreshing crab salad is a wonderful starter that also makes a stunning first course or main course for a light lunch. At the restaurant, our chefs typically use sweet, meaty Dungeness crab, found throughout California's coastal waters, but if you can't find Dungeness crab, any fresh crab will do. Keep in mind that most fishmongers sell cooked fresh crab that has been picked from the shell—a serious timesaver for the home cook. Crunchy fennel provides a delightful contrast to the crab, and the tangy rhubarb—macerated with strawberries and Madeira wine—offers an earthy flavor to marry with the seafood.

This intriguing dish includes five elements, but it's really not difficult to prepare; each step requires only 5 to 10 minutes of prep time, plus a little more for macerating, marinating, and simmering. The key here is organization: Take it step by step.

Enjoy with a crisp, unoaked Chardonnay; a bright, snappy Sauvignon Blanc; or a light, fresh dry rosé. And of course, sparkling wine would also be a fine choice.

10 ripe strawberries, hulled

1 rhubarb stalk, cut on the diagonal into 12 to 18 very thin slices

1 cup/240 ml Madeira wine

1 envelope (2½ tsp) unflavored gelatin

2 fennel bulbs, cores and stalks removed, 1 very thinly shaved and 1 cut into ½-in/ 12-mm dice, plus fennel fronds for garnish

5 tbsp/75 ml extra-virgin olive oil

2 tbsp fresh lemon juice

Salt

1 cup/30 g firmly packed baby spinach leaves

1 cup/240 ml Chicken Stock (page 216) or canned low-sodium chicken broth

¾ cup/180 ml heavy (whipping)/ double cream

1 lb/455 g fresh Dungeness or other lump crabmeat, picked over for shell fragments and cartilage

¼ cup/55 g crème fraîche

1 shallot, minced

2 tbsp chopped fresh chives

Freshly ground pepper

Put the strawberries in a bowl and mash them gently with a fork. Add the rhubarb slices to the bowl and pour in ½ cup/120 ml of the Madeira. Stir gently to mix and let stand at room temperature for about 1 hour. Strain through a fine-mesh sieve and discard the liquid. Return the macerated strawberry-rhubarb mixture to the bowl, cover, and refrigerate until ready to assemble.

In a saucepan, bring the remaining ½ cup/120 ml Madeira to a simmer over medium heat. Whisk in the gelatin until it dissolves. Pour the mixture into a nonreactive baking dish small enough so that the liquid covers the bottom in a thin film about ¼ in/6 mm thick. Refrigerate until the gelée sets, about 1 hour.

CONTINUED

Put the shaved fennel in a shallow, heatproof, nonreactive bowl. In a small saucepan, heat 3 tbsp of the olive oil over medium heat. Remove from the heat when the oil starts to shimmer or bubble slightly but before it begins to smoke. Pour the hot oil over the shaved fennel. Add 1 tbsp of the lemon juice and ½ tsp salt and stir to mix thoroughly. Let stand at room temperature for 30 minutes, then cover and refrigerate until ready to serve.

Bring a small saucepan three-fourths full of water to a boil over high heat. Add the spinach and cook just until tender, 30 to 45 seconds. Drain in a colander and immediately rinse under cold running water to halt the cooking. Drain again completely. Using your hands, squeeze the excess moisture from the spinach and set aside.

In a medium sauté pan or frying pan, heat 1 tbsp of the remaining olive oil over medium heat. Add the diced fennel and reduce the heat to medium-low. Cook, stirring occasionally, until the fennel is soft and translucent, about 20 minutes. Raise the heat to medium. Add the stock, bring to a simmer, and cook until most of the liquid has evaporated, about 5 minutes. Add the cream, bring to a simmer, and cook to heat the cream throughout and allow the flavors to blend, about 2 minutes longer. Transfer the creamed fennel to a blender or food processor, add the spinach, and pulse until the mixture is well combined and smooth. Remove any large pieces of fennel that may remain. Season with salt. Cover and refrigerate until well chilled, about 1 hour.

In a large, nonreactive bowl, combine the crabmeat, the remaining 1 tbsp olive oil and 1 tbsp lemon juice, the crème fraîche, shallot, and chives and fold gently to mix. Season with salt and pepper. Refrigerate until ready to serve.

To assemble the salads, spread a circle of the fennel sauce about 3 in/7.5 cm in diameter in the center of each serving plate. Place 2 slices of the strawberry-soaked rhubarb on top of the sauce, or slightly off-center. Using an ice-cream scoop, a mold, or a measuring cup and dividing it evenly, place a mound of the crab salad on top of the rhubarb. Arrange a few slices of the shaved fennel on top of the crab-salad mounds, and garnish with 1 more slice of rhubarb on the side. Using a fork, scrape up and crumble the chilled, set Madeira gelée. Arrange ½ tsp of gelée on each plate at the outer edge of each ring of fennel sauce. Garnish with the fennel fronds and serve at once.

shrimp ceviche salad

with melon, apple, and fresh ginger

This cornucopia of flavors comes together beautifully in an exotic, mouthwatering manner. Sweet, orange cantaloupe/rock melon offers a pleasing color contrast to the citrus-cured, porcelain white shrimp/prawns as well as a balance of tastes. The natural acidity in the lime juice changes the structure of the protein in the shellfish, basically cooking it without heat. To create pretty ribbons of apple and melon, it's easiest to use a vegetable peeler to shave them thinly. Jazzy ginger, tart apple, and fresh basil create more excitement on the palate.

With such diversity on your plate, sparkling wine holds the key to pleasure in your glass.

FOR THE CEVICHE:

6 tbsp/90 ml fresh lime juice

2 tsp chopped lime zest

2 tbsp extra-virgin olive oil

2 tsp salt

10 large shrimp/prawns, peeled, deveined, and cut into ½-in/12-mm dice

FOR THE DRESSING:

1 tbsp fresh lemon juice

1 tbsp fresh lime juice

¼ cup/60 ml extra-virgin olive oil

1 large shallot, minced

Salt

½ tart green apple such as Granny Smith, cut into ½-in/12-mm wedges or shaved into ribbons about 2 in/5 cm long

¼ cantaloupe/rockmelon, cut into ½-in/ 12-mm wedges and shaved into ribbons about 2 in/5 cm long (about ½ cup/85 g), plus 4 thin wedges, rinds removed

5 medium radishes, thinly sliced

¼ cup/7 g minced fresh basil

1 tbsp peeled and minced fresh ginger

Freshly ground pepper

TO MAKE THE CEVICHE: In a medium, nonreactive bowl, combine the lime juice and zest, olive oil, and salt. Whisk to blend thoroughly. Add the shrimp/prawns and stir to coat with the marinade. Let marinate at room temperature for 1 hour, stirring every 10 to 15 minutes.

TO MAKE THE DRESSING: While the ceviche is marinating, in a large, nonreactive bowl, combine the lemon juice, lime juice, olive oil, shallot, and salt to taste. Stir and let stand at room temperature for at least 10 minutes and up to 1 hour.

Just before serving, add the apple, ribboned cantaloupe/rockmelon, radishes, basil, and ginger to the bowl with the dressing and toss to mix well. Using a slotted spoon, transfer the shrimp from the marinade to the bowl. (Discard the marinade.) Toss thoroughly.

Place a melon wedge on each of 4 salad plates. Divide the salad evenly among the plates, nestling it into the curve of the melon wedges. Season with pepper and serve at once.

crab and corn bisque
with chervil oil

This hearty soup is teeming with fresh garden flavors and hints of the sea. It's topped with chervil oil and a fresh chervil garnish—both of which add a subtle, special touch. Chervil is an anise-flavored herb that can be found in most quality produce sections. If you can't find it, try using fresh tarragon as a substitute.

In California, the sweet meat from native Dungeness crab is our first choice here. But feel free to use any available fresh crabmeat. At the restaurant, our chefs often add an additional mound of crabmeat at the soup's center, but this version is sure to satisfy any lover of sweet, briny crustaceans.

A crisp white wine, such as Chardonnay, Sauvignon Blanc, Pinot Blanc, or Pinot Grigio, will work well in your glass. But we have a fondness for pairing crab with bubbly, a wine that quickly transforms this creamy chowder into a bona fide crab fest.

½ cup/15 g fresh chervil leaves, plus 2 tbsp

½ cup/120 ml extra-virgin olive oil, plus 2 tbsp

1 leek, white part only, cut into rounds ¼ in/ 6 mm thick and rinsed and drained thoroughly

1 yellow onion, diced

3 garlic cloves, minced

½ jalapeño chile, seeded and minced

2 medium white potatoes, peeled and diced

1 red bell pepper/capsicum, seeded and diced

3 cups/720 ml Chicken Stock (page 216) or canned low-sodium chicken broth

1 bottle (8 oz/240 ml) clam juice

1 cup/240 ml dry white wine

Salt

4 ears fresh corn, husks and silks removed

1 lb/455 g fresh Dungeness or other lump crabmeat, picked over for shell fragments and cartilage

½ cup/120 ml heavy (whipping)/ double cream

Freshly ground pepper

In a small sauté pan or frying pan over medium-low heat, combine the ½ cup/15 g chervil leaves with the ½ cup/120 ml olive oil and cook, stirring occasionally, until the oil is hot and small bubbles form around the edges, 3 to 5 minutes. Remove from the heat and let stand at room temperature for 1 hour. Strain the chervil-infused oil through a fine-mesh sieve and reserve. Discard the chervil.

In a soup pot, heat the 2 tbsp olive oil over medium heat. Add the leek and sauté until soft, about 3 minutes. Stir in the onion, garlic, and jalapeño. Sauté until the onion is translucent, about 3 minutes. Add the potatoes and bell pepper/capsicum and sauté for 3 minutes longer. Add the stock, clam juice, wine, and 1 tsp salt and stir to mix well. Raise the heat to high and bring to a boil, then reduce the heat to low, cover, and simmer until the potatoes are tender, about 10 minutes.

Meanwhile, cut the kernels from the ears of the corn. Add the corn kernels to the soup and simmer until the corn is tender, about 5 minutes. Add the crab and cook for 2 minutes to heat through. Stir in the cream and remove from the heat. Season with salt and pepper.

Ladle the bisque into warmed bowls. Swirl ½ to 1 tsp chervil oil into each serving and garnish with the 2 tbsp chervil leaves. Serve hot.

green vegetable gazpacho
with tiger shrimp and pickled red onions

This fragrant, refreshing summertime soup offers an appetizing mix of colors in your bowl. Copper-toned, striped tiger shrimp/prawns are topped with pink pickled onions, all neatly framed by a green-hued gazpacho filled with fresh vegetable flavors. Tomatillos, or Mexican green tomatoes, are easy to find in most supermarkets today, and add a savory but bright, melonlike quality to dishes. Peel away their papery husks, if still present (some stores remove them for you), and use warm water when rinsing to help dissolve the sticky film on the skins.

Using English hothouse cucumbers spares you the trouble of peeling and seeding, and the dark green skins add to the eye-catching appeal of the gazpacho. Consider setting knives alongside the spoons for this cold soup, as the large, meaty shellfish are more easily eaten when cut into bite-size morsels.

Serve with a chilled sparkling wine or dry rosé.

FOR THE GAZPACHO:

4 medium ripe tomatoes

6 cups/1.4 l Vegetable Stock (page 215) or canned low-sodium vegetable broth

1 English/hothouse cucumber, diced (about 2 cups/280 g)

1 green bell pepper/capsicum, seeded and diced

½ fennel bulb, diced (about 1 cup/140 g)

½ cup/55 g diced red onion

4 tomatillos, husked, rinsed, and diced

½ cup/15 g coarsely chopped fresh cilantro/ fresh coriander

2 avocados, pitted, peeled, and diced

2 garlic cloves, minced

Juice of ½ lime

Salt and freshly ground pepper

FOR THE PICKLED ONIONS:

1 cup/240 ml seasoned rice wine vinegar

¼ cup/50 g sugar

½ tsp black peppercorns

½ tsp fennel seeds

½ tsp coriander seeds

1 cinnamon stick

1 star anise pod

1 red onion, peeled and cut into ¼-in/ 6-mm rings

FOR THE SHRIMP/PRAWNS:

2 cups/480 ml dry white wine

3 tsp salt

1 yellow onion, peeled and quartered

1 medium leek, white part only, quartered and rinsed and drained thoroughly

1 carrot, peeled and cut into 2-in/5-cm pieces

18 tiger shrimp/prawns or other large variety, peeled and deveined

TO MAKE THE GAZPACHO: In a blender or food processor, combine the tomatoes and 2 cups/480 ml of the stock and process to a smooth purée. Strain the purée through a fine-mesh sieve into a large, nonreactive bowl. (Wait a few minutes to allow all the liquid to drain out.) Reserve this "tomato water" and discard the solids.

CONTINUED

In the blender or food processor, working in batches if necessary, combine the cucumber, bell pepper/capsicum, fennel, red onion, tomatillos, cilantro/fresh coriander, avocados, garlic, lime juice, and the remaining 4 cups/960 ml stock. Process to a coarse purée; the finished soup should contain small bits of crunchy fennel and cucumber. Transfer to a large bowl, add the reserved tomato water, and stir to mix well. Season with salt and pepper. Cover and refrigerate until well chilled, at least 1 hour or up to 24 hours.

TO MAKE THE PICKLED ONIONS: In a medium saucepan, combine the vinegar, sugar, peppercorns, fennel seeds, coriander seeds, cinnamon stick, and star anise. Bring to a boil over medium heat, stirring to dissolve the sugar. Simmer for 15 minutes. Strain through a fine-mesh sieve into a heatproof bowl or glass measuring jar. Discard the solids and return the liquid to the saucepan. Return to a simmer and add the onion, stirring them in the hot liquid for 1 minute. Remove the onion with tongs or drain in a colander. Discard the liquid. Put the onion in a bowl and refrigerate until ready to serve.

TO MAKE THE SHRIMP/PRAWNS: In a large pot, combine the wine, salt, onion, leek, carrot, and 8 cups/2 l water. Bring to a boil over high heat. Reduce the heat to medium-low and simmer for 30 minutes. Strain the liquid through a fine-mesh sieve into a large, heatproof bowl or another pot. Discard the solids. Return the liquid to the pot and bring to a simmer again. Prepare a large bowl of ice water and set aside. Place the shrimp/prawns in the simmering liquid and cook until they turn pink, about 2 minutes. Drain in a colander or remove them from the hot liquid with a slotted spoon. Immediately plunge the shellfish in the ice water bath and let cool for about 5 minutes, adding more ice if needed to keep the bath cold. Discard the cooking liquid. Once the meat is cool, remove and discard the tail fins.

Place 3 shrimp/prawns in each of 6 chilled bowls, with their curved shapes interlocked in what resembles a chain. Ladle the chilled gazpacho around the shellfish, but don't fill the bowls too high—you want to leave the tops of the crustaceans exposed and emerging from the soup. Garnish with a small mound of pickled red onions. Serve at once.

sunchoke soup
with shiitake mushrooms and crème fraîche

Sharing a certain earthiness, sunchokes and mushrooms have a special affinity. Sunchokes are potatolike sunflower tubers, sometimes called Jerusalem artichokes because their flavor and texture resembles that of an artichoke heart. This soup has a rich, smoky, down-to-earth character, but is still light enough to leave plenty of room for a second course. The restaurant's chefs use wild porcini mushrooms when they're in season, but shiitakes, available year-round, add their own special, buttery touch.

4 tbsp/60 ml extra-virgin olive oil

1 yellow onion, diced

2 leeks, white parts only, cut into rounds ¼ in/6 mm thick and rinsed and drained thoroughly

2 celery stalks, diced

2 lb/910 g sunchokes, peeled and cut into ½-in/12-mm dice

1 cup/240 ml dry white wine

4 cups/960 ml Chicken Stock (page 216) or canned low-sodium chicken broth

1 tsp salt

1 shallot, minced

2 garlic cloves, minced

8 oz/225 g shiitake mushrooms, brushed clean and thinly sliced

½ cup/120 ml heavy (whipping)/ double cream

¼ cup/55 g crème fraîche

Freshly ground pepper

In a soup pot, heat 2 tbsp of the olive oil over medium heat. Add the onion and sauté until translucent, about 2 minutes. Add the leeks and sauté until softened, about 2 minutes. Add the celery and sunchokes and sauté until tender, about 5 minutes longer.

Add the wine, stock, and salt and stir to blend. Raise the heat to high and bring to a boil. Reduce the heat to medium-low, cover, and simmer until the sunchokes are tender, about 15 minutes. Remove from the heat and let cool for 5 to 10 minutes. Transfer the soup to a blender or food processor, working in batches if necessary, and process to a smooth purée. Return the soup to the pot, cover, and set aside.

In a sauté pan or frying pan, heat the remaining 2 tbsp olive oil over medium heat. Add the shallot and garlic and sauté until fragrant, about 30 seconds. Stir in the mushrooms and sauté until they release their liquid and are tender, about 5 minutes. (If needed, add 1 to 2 tbsp water to the pan to prevent burning.)

Add the cream to the soup and reheat gently over medium-low heat. Taste and adjust the seasoning. Ladle the soup into warmed bowls. Garnish with the mushroom mixture, a dollop of crème fraîche, and freshly ground pepper. Serve hot.

cauliflower soup
with fried oysters and curry oil

This creamy soup is filled with flavors from both the garden and the sea. It also provides a beautiful visual presentation, with green chives and amber-hued curry oil dotting the soup's surface and tender, golden fried oysters afloat at the center. Note that the recipe calls for *panko*. These bread crumbs from Japanese cuisine are made from bread without crusts and are therefore crisper and lighter. They can be found in the Asian section of most well-stocked supermarkets.

As a perfect foil in your glass, enjoy a tangy, chilled sparkling wine or a light-bodied Chardonnay or Sauvignon Blanc.

1 tbsp curry powder

3 tbsp canola oil, plus 1 cup/240 ml

2 tbsp unsalted butter

2 bacon/streaky bacon slices, cut crosswise into matchsticks about ¼ in/6 mm thick

1 yellow onion, diced

2 garlic cloves, minced

1 large head cauliflower, cored and cut into 2-in/5-cm pieces (about 4 cups/455 g)

3 cups/720 ml Chicken Stock (page 216) or canned low-sodium chicken broth

1 cup/240 ml heavy (whipping)/ double cream

¼ tsp salt

¼ cup/30 g all-purpose/plain flour

¼ cup/30 g *panko* bread crumbs

1 large egg, lightly beaten

12 fresh medium oysters, shucked

2 tbsp chopped fresh chives

In a small, dry frying pan, toast the curry powder over medium heat until fragrant, about 1 minute. Add the 3 tbsp of canola oil and stir to blend thoroughly. Remove from the heat and set aside at room temperature.

In a soup pot, melt the butter over medium heat. Add the bacon and sauté until crisp, about 3 minutes. Add the onion and garlic and sauté until the onion is translucent, about 3 minutes. Add the cauliflower, stock, cream, and salt and stir to blend. Bring to a boil over high heat. Reduce the heat to medium-low and simmer, stirring occasionally, until the cauliflower is tender, about 20 minutes. Remove from the heat and let cool for 5 to 10 minutes. Transfer the soup to a blender or food processor, working in batches if necessary, and process to a smooth purée. Return the soup to the pot, cover, and set aside.

In a small frying pan, heat the 1 cup/240 ml of canola oil over high heat until it begins to shimmer or show little bubbles around the edges but before it begins to smoke. While the oil is heating, put the flour, bread crumbs, and beaten egg in three separate small, shallow bowls.

When the oil is hot, work quickly to prepare the oysters. Dredge 3 or 4 oysters at a time in the flour, dip them in the egg, and then coat them in the bread crumbs. Using tongs, chopsticks, or a slotted spoon, gently place the oysters in the pan, being careful not to splatter the hot oil or crowd the pan. Fry until golden brown, about 1 minute per side. Transfer the fried oysters to a plate lined with paper towels/absorbent papers to drain. Let the oil return to shimmering-hot and repeat to fry the remaining oysters.

Reheat the soup over medium-low heat. Ladle into warmed bowls and arrange 2 oysters in the middle of each serving. Drizzle with the curry oil and garnish with the chives. Serve hot.

sugar pie pumpkin soup
with glazed chestnuts

With festive cinnamon and nutmeg spices, this creamy soup is a heavenly incarnation of a savory pumpkin pie. Sugar pie pumpkins are commonly found in supermarkets during the fall and winter months. They are smaller than your typical jack-o'-lantern—and sweeter, too—which makes them better for cooking. Crunchy chestnuts add texture, highlighted by a touch of smoky bacon. A finishing swirl of crème fraîche tops it all off with elegance.

This rich soup is a perfect partner for spicy, fruity, and perhaps slightly sweet wines. A big, buttery Chardonnay could bring out the best in this soup. Gewürztraminer and Riesling, made in both dry and sweet styles, are also excellent choices here. If you're looking for something lighter, try a sparkling Crémant or Chandon's own Riche, made with very subtle sweetness.

1 small sugar pie pumpkin (3 to 4 lb/1.4 to 1.8 kg)	1 yellow onion, diced
5 tbsp/70 g unsalted butter	1 tbsp ground cinnamon
3 tbsp brown sugar/demerara sugar	4 fresh sage leaves or ½ tsp dried sage
½ tsp freshly grated nutmeg	½ cup/120 ml heavy (whipping)/ double cream
8 chestnuts	Salt and freshly ground pepper
1 bacon/streaky bacon slice, diced	6 tsp crème fraîche
1 shallot, minced	
6 cups/1.4 l Chicken Stock (page 216) or canned low-sodium chicken broth	

Preheat the oven to 400°F/200°C/gas 6.

Cut the pumpkin into three large pieces. Using a large metal spoon, remove the seeds and stringy pumpkin surface flesh and discard both. Divide 2 tbsp of the butter into three equal portions and place one portion in the center of the flesh side of each pumpkin piece. Sprinkle 1 tbsp of the brown sugar/demerara sugar onto each pumpkin piece and sprinkle each with one-third of the nutmeg. Place the pumpkin pieces on a baking sheet/tray, cover each with aluminum foil, and bake until tender, about 1½ hours.

While the pumpkin is baking, prepare the chestnuts. Score each chestnut by poking the tip of a paring knife into the nut just above the base. Gently press the knife down to pierce the shell, making an incision about ½ in/12 mm long. Repeat on the opposite side of the base of the chestnut. Alternatively, use a serrated knife to cut an X in the top, or round part, of each chestnut. The point is to create an opening that allows steam to escape from the roasting nut. Chestnuts can be hard and slippery, so be careful not to let the knife blade slip while you work.

Place all of the scored chestnuts in a small, dry frying pan and heat over high heat for about 1 minute. Using tongs, turn the chestnuts and cook for 1 minute on the second side. They will turn slightly darker. Remove the hot chestnuts from the pan, wrap them in a paper towel/absorbent paper, and use the palm of your hand to gently press on the chestnuts and crack them. Peel the shells and skins off the chestnuts while they are still warm. Chop the meat coarsely and set aside.

In the same small frying pan, sauté the bacon over medium heat until crisp, about 3 minutes. Stir in the shallot and chopped chestnut. Add 1 cup/240 ml of the stock and 1 tbsp of the butter. When the mixture begins to bubble, reduce the heat to medium-low and simmer until the liquid evaporates, about 15 minutes. Remove from the heat and set aside.

When the pumpkin is tender and easily pierced with a fork, remove from the oven, remove the foil, and let cool for 15 minutes. Use the metal spoon to scrape out the pumpkin flesh into a bowl and set aside. (Discard the pumpkin skin.) In a soup pot, melt the remaining 2 tbsp butter over medium heat. Add the onion and sauté until translucent, about 3 minutes. Add the cinnamon and sage and stir thoroughly. Add the remaining 5 cups/1.2 l stock, the cream, pumpkin, and salt and pepper to taste. Raise the heat to high and bring to a boil. Reduce the heat to low and simmer for 15 minutes to allow the flavors to blend. Transfer the soup to a blender or food processor, working in batches if necessary, and process to a very smooth purée. Return the soup to the pot and reheat over medium-low heat.

Ladle the soup into warmed bowls. Garnish each portion with about 1 tbsp of the glazed chestnuts and swirl 1 tsp of the crème fraîche around the chestnut garnish. Serve hot.

pastas and grains, plus one

With their uncanny ability to serve as a foil for so many differently styled sauces and other foods, grains and pastas provide a bedrock component to nearly every culinary culture. Simply put, these diversely shaped and textured carbohydrates carry flavor with great efficiency. At the restaurant, we generally use grains and pastas in a creative dynamic that pairs them in a supporting role to the star of a main course, such as the fish in Striped Bass with Forbidden Black Rice and Chorizo or the pork in Pork Loin Chops with Ricotta Gnocchi in Sage Butter.

But sometimes, we find that a particular grain or pasta dish is distinguished by its ability to stand on its own as a first course, a main course, or possibly a side dish. The ricotta gnocchi mentioned above might also serve as such an example, although we typically pair it with the pork loin chops indicated in the recipe. Risotto and many pastas, on the other hand, are traditionally stand-alone items. You'll find Foie Gras Risotto, for example, to be so intriguing as a solo act that just about any accompaniment would pale by comparison. As a result, we have included a number of these exceptional recipes here in their own chapter.

Another widely appreciated carbohydrate—the potato—shares the culinary versatility inherent in grains and pastas. It's no wonder that a comfort-food classic like the Three-Cheese Potato Gratin would share the niche in this chapter as well.

Each recipe featured here has its own personality and particular affinity for interesting wine-pairing opportunities. Enjoy these dishes alone in the spirit of independence, or served as an introduction or a digression to a broader prandial vision.

recipes

rice noodles
with stir-fried vegetables and cilantro-lime dressing

This heartwarming dish presents a colorful vegetable display framed by silky white rice noodles. There are many kinds of rice noodles used in Asian cooking, any of which will work here, but we recommend the wide, flat Asian noodles sometimes labeled rice vermicelli—not to be confused with the thin Italian wheat noodles sporting the same name. The wider and flatter the noodle, the better it will hold the sauce. Note that rice noodles cook in about half the time it takes to cook most Italian-style wheat-based noodles.

These noodles are loaded with bright flavors and topped with a crunchy peanut garnish. Fresh ginger and jalapeño give extra lift. And as long as you're adept with chopping, you'll find this quick-cooking stir-fry particularly easy to prepare.

Sparkling wine or any other crisp, white still wine will pair nicely here. Or pour fresh-brewed green tea over ice, an equally perfect beverage match.

FOR THE DRESSING:

2 tbsp minced fresh cilantro/fresh coriander

1 tbsp peeled and minced fresh ginger

½ jalapeño chile, seeded and minced

1 garlic clove, minced

¼ cup/60 ml soy sauce

Juice of 1 lime

3 tbsp water

1 tsp sugar

Salt

½ lb/225 g Asian flat rice (vermicelli) noodles

2 cups/170 g bean sprouts

½ English/hothouse cucumber, diced (about 1 cup/140 g)

1 cup/30 g coarsely chopped romaine/ Cos lettuce

2 tbsp minced fresh mint

2 tbsp canola oil

1 small white onion, diced

2 cups/115 g broccoli florets

2 cups/170 g firmly packed shredded napa cabbage

1 carrot, peeled and cut into thin rounds

1 red bell pepper/capsicum, seeded and cut into thin strips

3 tbsp soy sauce

5 green/spring onions, white parts only, chopped

3 tbsp peanuts, toasted (see page 212) and chopped

TO MAKE THE DRESSING: In a medium bowl, combine the cilantro/fresh coriander, ginger, jalapeño, and garlic. Using a wooden spoon, stir to mix well. Stir in the soy sauce, lime juice, water, and sugar. Stir until well mixed and the sugar has dissolved. Set aside.

Bring a large pot three-fourths full of lightly salted water to a boil over high heat. Add the noodles and cook until tender, 5 to 7 minutes. Drain in a colander, rinse briefly under cold running water, and shake to drain completely. Transfer the noodles to a large bowl and add the bean sprouts, cucumber, lettuce, and mint. Cover and set aside.

In a wok or large frying pan, heat the canola oil over medium heat. Add the white onion and sauté until translucent, 2 to 3 minutes. Add the broccoli, cabbage, carrot, and bell pepper/capsicum. Stir to mix well. To prevent burning, add 2 to 3 tbsp water and stir again. Cover and continue to cook, stirring occasionally, until the vegetables are tender, 3 to 4 minutes longer. Remove from the heat and stir in the soy sauce.

Add the rice noodle mixture to the pan with the vegetables and toss to mix well. Pour the dressing over the noodles and toss again. Divide the noodles and vegetables among pasta bowls or dinner plates. Garnish each serving with the green/spring onions and the toasted peanuts. Serve at once.

serves 6
as a first course,
4 as a main
course

fettuccini
with spicy red pepper and tomato sauce

Traditional tomato sauces pale next to this version, made with a large proportion of sweet, roasted red peppers/capsicums. The sauce coats the broad fettuccini noodles amply and will please anyone who appreciates robust, original flavors.

The dish delivers a bit of heat—but not too much—that comes from the *piment d'Espelette*, a spicy pepper grown in the southern French town of its name. Look for the paprika-like spice powder in most specialty-food shops. If you can't find it, any hot paprika, such as New Mexico red chile powder, will work fine.

Pair this pasta with a spicy red Zinfandel or a chilled, unoaked Chardonnay or herbal Sauvignon Blanc.

2 tbsp extra-virgin olive oil

3 garlic cloves, minced

3 red bell peppers/capsicums, roasted, peeled, and seeded (see page 212) and cut into strips ½ in/12 mm wide

2 medium tomatoes, diced

2 tbsp grated lemon zest

3 fresh thyme sprigs, each about 4 in/10 cm long

1 tsp *piment d'Espelette* or other hot paprika such as New Mexico red chile powder

Salt

½ cup/120 ml dry white wine

½ cup/120 ml Chicken Stock (page 216) or canned low-sodium chicken broth

Freshly ground black pepper

1 lb/455 g dried fettuccini pasta

⅓ cup/45 g freshly grated Parmesan cheese

In a large saucepan or frying pan, heat the olive oil over medium heat. Add the garlic and sauté until fragrant, about 30 seconds. Add the roasted peppers/capsicums and tomatoes and sauté for 5 minutes, stirring occasionally. Add the lemon zest, thyme, *piment d'Espelette*, and ½ tsp salt and stir to mix thoroughly. Sauté for 5 minutes longer. Raise the heat to medium-high. Stir in the wine and stock, bring to a simmer, and cook for 5 minutes more to allow the flavors to blend. (Reduce the heat to medium if the sauce begins to boil too aggressively.) Remove and discard the thyme sprigs.

Transfer the mixture to a blender or food processor, working in batches if necessary, and process to a smooth purée. Return the purée to the original pan and simmer over medium-low heat, stirring frequently, until the sauce has thickened and most of the liquid has evaporated, about 5 minutes. Taste and adjust the seasoning with salt and black pepper. Remove from the heat and cover to keep warm.

Bring a large pot three-fourths full of lightly salted water to a boil over high heat. Add the pasta and cook until tender but still firm to the bite (al dente), about 10 minutes. Drain in a colander but do not rinse; shake the colander to drain excess water.

Quickly reheat the sauce over medium-high heat. Add the pasta to the pan and toss until evenly coated with the sauce. Divide the pasta among warmed plates or pasta bowls and sprinkle with the Parmesan. Serve at once.

serves 6
as a first course,
4 as a main
course

creamy sunchoke risotto

Also known as Jerusalem artichokes, sunchokes impart a subtle taste not unlike their namesake's to this creamy, golden risotto. Even when thoroughly cooked, sunchokes provide a bit of fresh-tasting crunchiness to any recipe. This classic risotto, distinguished by the use of sparkling wine in place of still, which delivers a delicate twist on the palate, makes a fine first course or a light main course.

Arborio rice is a short-grained Italian rice named for the town where it is grown. Blessed with a high starch content, it is particularly creamy and chewy—two characteristics that make it an ideal flavor vector. Arborio rice is widely available in specialty-food shops and most fine supermarkets.

You'll have more than a half-bottle of bubbly left after cooking, so keep the rest chilled for drinking.

2 tbsp unsalted butter

1½ lb/680 g sunchokes, peeled and thinly sliced

1½ cups/360 ml heavy (whipping)/double cream

3 tbsp extra-virgin olive oil

1 yellow onion, finely chopped

1 cup/215 g Arborio rice

4½ cups/1 l Vegetable Stock (page 215) or canned low-sodium vegetable broth, plus more if needed

1 cup/240 ml sparkling wine such as Chandon Brut Classic

½ cup/60 g freshly grated Parmesan cheese

¼ cup/7 g minced fresh chives

Salt and freshly ground pepper

In a large sauté pan or frying pan over medium heat, melt the butter. Add the sunchokes, stir to coat evenly with the butter, and sauté until they begin to turn golden, about 5 minutes. Shake the pan occasionally to prevent burning. Add the cream and stir until it begins to simmer. Reduce the heat to low and cook, stirring occasionally, until the sunchokes are tender and easily pierced with a fork, 30 to 35 minutes.

Transfer the creamed sunchokes to a blender or food processor, working in batches if necessary, and process to a very smooth purée. You should have about 2 cups/455 g sunchoke purée. Set aside.

In a large, deep sauté pan or a Dutch oven, heat the olive oil over medium heat. Add the onion and sauté until translucent, about 3 minutes. Add the rice and, using a wooden spoon, stir until the grains are evenly coated with the oil, 2 to 3 minutes. Add ½ cup/120 ml of the stock and cook, stirring frequently, until most of the liquid is absorbed, about 3 minutes. Continue the process in ½-cup additions, alternating the stock and the wine, until all the wine has been absorbed. Add the remaining stock, still ½ cup at a time, until all the liquid has been absorbed and the rice is tender but still slightly firm at the center of each grain, about 30 minutes total. Add a little more stock to finish cooking the rice, if needed.

Add the sunchoke purée and Parmesan to the rice and stir to mix thoroughly. Cook, stirring, until the cheese melts and the mixture thickens, about 5 minutes. Remove from the heat and stir in the chives. Season with salt and pepper. Divide the risotto among warmed plates; serve at once.

serves 6
as a first course,
4 as a main
course

foie gras risotto

Foie gras is incredibly rich—famously rich. But this dish, a blend of French and Italian culinary traditions, captures the experience of the world's most luxurious liver with a light touch. Perfect as an appetizer, this silky-savory risotto can also serve as a main course.

In either case, we recommend a distinctive white or red wine with good acidity as an accompaniment. Sparkling wine has a natural affinity for foie gras, as do barrel-fermented Chardonnay or Viognier among still whites. Pinot Noir and Syrah would make excellent red-wine pairings. An off-dry white Riesling could well add an interesting dimension to the dining experience.

½ cup/120 ml heavy (whipping)/ double cream

4 to 6 oz/115 to 170 g fresh foie gras, cut into ½-in/12-mm dice

2 tbsp extra-virgin olive oil

1 tbsp unsalted butter

½ yellow onion, finely chopped

1 shallot, minced

1 cup/215 g Arborio rice

3½ cups/840 ml Chicken Stock (page 216) or canned low-sodium chicken broth, plus more if needed

1 cup/240 ml dry white wine

Salt and freshly ground pepper

¼ cup/30 g freshly grated Parmesan cheese

In a small saucepan over medium heat, warm the cream until steam begins to rise. Do not let boil. Remove from the heat. In a blender or food processor, combine the hot cream and the foie gras and process to a smooth purée. Cover and set aside.

In a large, deep sauté pan or a Dutch oven, heat the olive oil and butter over medium heat. When the butter has melted, add the onion and shallot and sauté until translucent, about 3 minutes. Add the rice and, using a wooden spoon, stir until the grains are evenly coated with the butter and oil, 2 to 3 minutes.

Add ½ cup/120 ml of the stock and cook, stirring frequently, until most of the liquid is absorbed, about 3 minutes. Add ½ cup/120 ml of the wine and cook, stirring frequently, until most of the liquid is absorbed, about 3 minutes. Continue the process in ½-cup/120-ml additions, alternating the stock and the wine, until all the wine has been absorbed. Add the remaining stock, still ½ cup/120 ml at a time, until all the liquid has been absorbed and the rice is tender but still slightly firm at the center of each grain, about 30 minutes total. Add a little more stock to finish cooking the rice, if needed.

Reduce the heat to medium-low, pour the foie gras purée into the risotto, and stir constantly until most of the purée is absorbed by the rice, 2 to 3 minutes.

Remove from the heat. Season with salt and pepper. Divide the risotto among warmed plates or pasta bowls. Garnish with the Parmesan and serve at once.

three-cheese potato gratin

serves 4 as
a main course, 6
to 8 as
a side dish

This French classic takes on a decidedly international flavor with three cheeses: earthy French Gruyère, nutty Italian Parmesan, and tangy Danish Havarti. Together they bring a wealth of character to the dish, which emerges from the oven bubbly hot and needs a few minutes to settle and solidify.

The golden-topped, creamy gratin makes a fine main course on its own, especially when preceded by an interesting appetizer or salad. But, of course, these potatoes are also a natural as a side dish— perhaps best suited to simply prepared meats such as beef tenderloin or pork loin chops, featured in these pages with truffled mashed potatoes and ricotta gnocchi, respectively. Try the substitutions to add variety to your repertoire.

Be sure to slice the potatoes as thinly as possible, or they may not cook evenly. A mandoline or food processor fitted with the slicing blade is typically well suited to the task, but a large, sharp knife in careful, patient hands is also quite effective.

A rich dish such as this one marries well with many kinds of wine. Chardonnay, Riesling, and Roussanne might top your list of potential whites. Light, fruity Pinot Noir or Pinot Meunier would serve well among reds.

1 tbsp unsalted butter	3 lb/1.4 kg white potatoes, peeled and thinly sliced
2 cups/480 ml heavy (whipping)/ double cream	½ cup/55 g freshly shredded Havarti cheese
½ tsp salt	¼ cup/30 g freshly shredded Gruyère cheese
¼ tsp freshly ground pepper	¼ cup/30 g freshly grated Parmesan cheese
¼ tsp freshly grated nutmeg	

Preheat the oven to 350°F/180°C/gas 4. Grease an 8-in/20-cm square baking dish with the butter.

In a bowl, whisk together the cream, salt, pepper, and nutmeg. On the bottom of the prepared dish, place one-fourth of the potato slices in a layer about ¼ in/6 mm thick. Pour in ½ cup/120 ml of the cream mixture and sprinkle with one-fourth of the Havarti cheese. Repeat to make three more layers of potatoes, cream, and Havarti. Sprinkle the top layer with the Gruyere and Parmesan cheeses as well.

Bake until the potatoes are tender and the top is bubbly and golden brown, 45 to 50 minutes. Remove from the oven and let cool for 10 to 15 minutes to allow the gratin to firm up. Serve warm.

pastas and grains, plus one **117**

CHAPTER 6
seafood

To the casual traveler, Napa Valley may seem landlocked. But its proximity to the sea is critical to the valley's singular climate and suitability for fine-wine grape growing. The Pacific Ocean is only an hour's drive from the vines of Domaine Chandon. During the warm growing season, the chilly, indigo sea sends cooling maritime breezes inland, preserving natural acidity in our grapes to provide the finest quality fruit for our wines.

The nearby Pacific also supplies the restaurant with a steady supply of fresh fish and crustaceans. In the fall and winter, diners tuck into local Dungeness crab, featured in many dishes or enjoyed directly from the shell in the company of a glass of chilled Chandon Brut. Equally bubbly-friendly bivalves such as scallops and mussels inhabit the coastal waters. At low tide, you can see an endless array of bearded black mussels clinging to the rocky outcrops that hug the coastline. They are the inspiration for Coconut Lime Mussels.

Also at the edge of the sea, the region's most famous oyster farms lie in the narrow finger of water called Tomales Bay, where seals and great white sharks swim. The sharks and seals know where to find the best-tasting fish, and it's no accident these undersea hunters thrive off the Northern California coast. The items on their menu also grace ours at the restaurant; a day's catch may include tuna, salmon, halibut, skate, and sea bass, offering an array of textures and flavors to set off any chef's or home cook's imagination. Enjoy a coastal perspective as you dine on such dishes as Baked Salmon with Roasted Beets and Onion-Clove Purée or Striped Bass with Forbidden Black Rice and Chorizo. Regardless of where you may find yourself, a taste of the ocean is only a meal away.

recipes

coconut lime mussels

serves 6 to 8 as
an appetizer, 4 as
a main course

This tropical twist on the French classic *moules marinières* serves up briny mussels in a tangy coconut broth enhanced by ginger and lemongrass. You'll find the pretty green stalks of fresh lemongrass in the produce section of many fine supermarkets and specialty-food shops, alongside the brown knobby fresh ginger rhizomes, or roots. Both aromatics need to be peeled before using, and both have dense, stringy flesh that can be difficult to mince. Grating is a good solution for ginger; include the juices that are extruded when you scrape. For lemongrass, peel and use only the tender midsection of the slender, bulblike stalk. Smash it with the flat side of a chef's knife to make mincing easier.

Increase your dining pleasure by sipping, as an accompaniment, any bright, fresh white wine that offers good acidity. Think sparkling wine, unoaked Chardonnay, Pinot Grigio, or Sauvignon Blanc.

2 tbsp extra-virgin olive oil

2 shallots, minced

2 garlic cloves, minced

2 tsp peeled and grated fresh ginger

2 tsp minced lemongrass

3 tbsp fresh lime juice

2 cups/480 ml dry white wine

1 cup/240 ml unsweetened coconut milk

2 to 2½ lb/910 g to 1.2 kg mussels, scrubbed and debearded

2 tbsp minced fresh flat-leaf (Italian) parsley or scallions

In a large pot, heat the olive oil over medium-high heat. Add the shallots and sauté until translucent, about 2 minutes. Add the garlic, ginger, and lemongrass and stir to mix well. Simmer until fragrant, about 30 seconds. Stir in the lime juice. Add the wine and stir, using a wooden spoon to scrape up any browned bits that have stuck to the bottom of the pot.

Bring the wine mixture to a boil and cook for about 2 minutes. Reduce the heat to medium and stir in the coconut milk. Add the mussels to the pot, discarding any that do not close to the touch, and stir gently to coat them with the liquid. Cover and cook until all the shells have opened, about 5 minutes. Discard any mussels that remain closed.

Divide the mussels among warmed bowls and ladle in the hot broth. Garnish with the parsley or scallions and serve at once.

seared day-boat scallops
with porcini mushrooms and asparagus

Hand-harvested day-boat scallops are typically the freshest, sweetest, and most tender scallops you can buy. They are fairly large and filling; 3 or 4 should satisfy even the heartiest appetites. Scallops need to be seared quickly over a hot stovetop, allowing them to brown nicely on their exteriors. Be careful not to over-cook them, however, or they will turn rubbery. Inside, the flesh should remain soft and slightly translucent.

These scallops are dressed in a simple butter sauce while resting on a bed of mushrooms and asparagus. In winter, Domaine Chandon's chefs use wild, meaty porcini mushrooms, which grow in profusion on the nearby slopes of Mount Veeder. You can substitute any mushrooms—including common white button mushrooms—with excellent results.

Richly textured scallops in butter require an equally rich white wine as a pairing partner. Look for one that offers bright acidity as well. Barrel-fermented Chardonnay, fruity Riesling, and spicy Gewürztraminer would all make excellent choices. A slightly sweet sparkling wine like Crémant or Chandon Riche would also be worth investigating.

Salt

1 lb/455 g asparagus, hard ends trimmed away, cut into 3-in/7.5-cm lengths

4 tbsp/60 ml olive oil

8 oz/225 g fresh porcini or other mushrooms, brushed clean and sliced

2 garlic cloves, minced

1 shallot, minced

Freshly ground pepper

2 tbsp chopped fresh flat-leaf (Italian) parsley, plus whole leaves, for garnish

12 to 16 day-boat scallops

3 tbsp sherry vinegar

3 tbsp unsalted butter

Lemon zest for garnish (optional)

Bring a medium saucepan filled halfway with lightly salted water to a boil over high heat. Drop the asparagus into the hot water and cook until tender but still firm to the bite, about 3 minutes. Drain in a colander, rinse under cold running water, and set aside.

In a medium frying pan, heat 2 tbsp of the olive oil over medium-high heat. Add the mushrooms and sauté until they release their liquid and are tender, about 5 minutes. (If needed, add 1 to 2 tbsp water to the pan to prevent sticking or burning.) Add the garlic and shallot and cook, stirring occasionally, until translucent, 3 to 4 minutes longer. Season with salt and pepper. Add the asparagus and toss to mix with the mushrooms. Add the minced parsley and toss to mix. Remove from the heat and cover to keep warm.

CONTINUED

Lightly salt the scallops on both sides. In a large sauté pan or frying pan, heat the remaining 2 tbsp olive oil over high heat. When the oil begins to shimmer, reduce the heat to medium-high and arrange the scallops in the pan. Sear until browned on the first side, 1 to 2 minutes. Using tongs, carefully turn and sear until browned on the second side, about 1 minute longer. Continue to cook the scallops, turning occasionally to prevent sticking, 2 to 3 minutes longer. Take care not to overcook; the interior flesh should remain slightly translucent. Transfer the scallops to a plate and cover to keep warm.

Add the sherry vinegar to the pan and use a wooden spoon to scrape up any browned bits from the bottom of the pan. Reduce the heat to medium and add the butter, stirring occasionally as it melts. While the butter is melting, divide the asparagus mixture among warmed plates. Place 3 or 4 scallops on top of the vegetables. Drizzle any juices that collected on the plate holding the scallops back into the pan with the melted butter and stir to mix. Spoon the butter sauce over the scallops and vegetables. Garnish with parsley and lemon zest, if desired. Serve at once.

soft-shell crab tempura
with lemon-cayenne aioli

serves 6 to 8 as
a first course,
4 as a main
course

In the spring, blue crabs shed their hard outer shell and make it possible for us to enjoy eating them—soft shell and all. Fried in a crispy tempura batter and then dipped in a subtly spicy lemon aioli sauce, they make a fine first course or main course. When serving as a main course, count on 3 or 4 crabs per person.

In your glass, there is no better pairing than a cool, crisp bubbly.

FOR THE LEMON-CAYENNE AIOLI:
2 tsp Dijon mustard

1 large egg yolk, at room temperature

¼ cup/60 ml extra-virgin olive oil

¼ cup/60 ml canola oil

1 tbsp minced lemon zest

⅛ tsp cayenne pepper

1 tsp fresh lemon juice

Salt

Canola oil for deep-frying

1½ cups/195 g all-purpose/plain flour

½ cup/55 g cornstarch/cornflour

1 tsp salt

1 large egg yolk

1½ cups/360 ml cold water

12 to 16 soft-shell crabs, tails and gills removed

TO MAKE THE AIOLI: In a medium bowl, combine the mustard and egg yolk. Very gradually add the oils in a fine, steady stream, whisking until they emulsify into a pale yellow, thick sauce. Whisk in the lemon zest and cayenne. Add the lemon juice and whisk to blend thoroughly. Season with salt. Cover and refrigerate for up to 24 hours.

Pour canola oil into a large, deep, heavy sauté pan or frying pan to a depth of 1½ in/4 cm and heat over medium-high heat until it begins to shimmer or show little bubbles around the edges.

While the oil is heating, put 1 cup/130 g of the flour in a medium bowl and set aside. In another medium bowl, whisk together the remaining ½ cup/65 g flour, the cornstarch/cornflour, and the salt. In a large bowl, combine the egg yolk and cold water and whisk to blend thoroughly. Gradually add the flour-and-cornstarch mixture to the egg-yolk mixture, whisking until a smooth batter forms.

When the oil is hot, work quickly to prepare the crabs. Dredge the crabs in the plain flour and then immerse them in the batter. Using tongs, chopsticks, or a slotted spoon, gently place 6 to 8 crabs in the pan, being careful not to splatter the hot oil or crowd the pan. Fry until the batter is crisp and lightly golden on the first side, 2 to 3 minutes. Turn and fry until crisp on the second side. (Watch carefully, as the second side will cook more quickly than the first side—no more than 2 minutes.)

Transfer the fried crabs to a serving platter lined with paper towels/absorbent papers to drain. Serve at once with the aioli dipping sauce. Let the oil return to shimmering-hot and repeat to fry the remaining crabs.

lobster saffron cream sauce
and pappardelle noodles

serves 6
as a first course,
4 as a main
course

Saffron's exotic aroma is seductive. It adds spice and color to this rich, creamy sauce filled with sweet, tender lobster tail. Wide, flat pappardelle noodles carry the flavors beautifully, but other flat-noodle pasta can stand in as a substitute.

In your wineglass, fruity Riesling or Gewürztraminer makes an excellent match. So does a lush, full-bodied Chardonnay.

1¼ lb/570 g lobster tails (4 or 5 medium tails)	1 cup/240 ml dry white wine
Salt	½ tsp saffron
1 lb/455 g dried pappardelle pasta	1 cup/240 ml heavy (whipping)/ double cream
2 tbsp unsalted butter	
2 shallots, minced	Freshly ground pepper
2 garlic cloves, minced	2 tbsp minced fresh flat-leaf (Italian) parsley
Pinch of red pepper flakes	

Set a steamer basket in a large saucepan and add water to reach just below the bottom of the basket. Place the lobster tails in the steamer and bring the water to a boil over high heat. Reduce the heat to maintain a simmer and cover the pan. Steam just until the tails begin to turn light pink, about 3 minutes. (They should not be fully cooked, or they will become rubbery later on.) Using tongs, remove the tails from the steamer and let cool. Reserve 1 cup/240 ml of the steaming liquid in the pot and discard the rest.

When the lobster tails are cool enough to handle, use the point of a paring knife to score the underside of each tail crosswise in three or four places and cut a line lengthwise along the middle of each tail. Crack the tails open and pull out the meat. Chop it into small (about ½ in/12 mm) chunks and set aside.

Bring a large pot three-fourths full of lightly salted water to a boil over high heat. Add the pasta and stir it a bit as it softens. Reduce the heat slightly, but keep it high enough to maintain a boil without splattering the stove. Cook until the noodles are tender but still firm to the bite (al dente), 8 to 10 minutes. Drain in a colander but do not rinse; shake the colander to drain excess water. Leave the noodles in the colander and set aside.

While the pasta is cooking, in a large sauté pan or frying pan with deep sides, melt the butter over medium heat. Add the shallots and sauté for 1 minute. Add the garlic and red pepper flakes and cook until fragrant, about 30 seconds. Add the reserved steaming liquid, the wine, the saffron, and ¼ tsp salt. Raise the heat to high and bring to a boil. Reduce the heat to medium-high and simmer until the liquid has reduced by half, 8 to 10 minutes. Add the cream and continue to simmer, stirring occasionally, until the sauce thickens, about 4 minutes. Add the lobster chunks and cook for another 2 minutes to heat through. Remove from the heat.

Add the pasta to the pan and toss to coat the noodles thoroughly with the saffron sauce. Taste and adjust the seasoning with salt and pepper. Divide among warmed plates or pasta bowls, garnish with the parsley, and serve at once.

roasted halibut
with fresh corn porridge

Sweet summer corn provides a stage for flaky white halibut fillets in this simple, yet elegant, preparation. For best results, use the freshest corn you can find.

The buttery fish fillets and corn make an excellent match for an equally buttery Chardonnay or fruity Chenin Blanc or Viognier.

7 cups/1.2 kg fresh white or yellow corn kernels (from about 8 large ears of corn)

Salt

3 tbsp extra-virgin olive oil

1 medium white onion, cut into 8 to 10 cubes

4 tbsp/55 g unsalted butter

¼ cup/60 ml Vegetable Stock (page 215) or canned low-sodium vegetable broth, plus more if needed

1 tbsp minced lemon zest

1 tbsp minced fresh sage or ½ tsp dried sage

Freshly ground pepper

4 skinless halibut fillets, about 5 oz/140 g each

In a blender or food processor, process 5 cups/860 g of the corn kernels to a very smooth purée. Pour the purée through a fine-mesh sieve into a bowl, pushing down on the solids with the back of a large spoon to extract as much of the liquid as possible. Discard the solids and reserve the liquid, which should be about 1 cup/240 ml. Transfer the corn juice to a small saucepan and bring to a simmer over medium heat. Reduce the heat to low and simmer gently, stirring frequently, until the juice thickens, about 3 minutes. Remove from the heat and season with salt. Set aside.

In a large sauté pan or frying pan, heat 1 tbsp of the olive oil over medium heat. Add the onion and sauté until translucent, about 5 minutes. Add the remaining 2 cups/340 g corn and sauté for 2 minutes. Add the 2 tbsp of the butter, ¼ cup/60 ml stock, the lemon zest, and the sage and bring to a simmer. Cook until most of the liquid has evaporated, about 2 minutes. Taste and adjust the seasoning with salt and pepper. Remove the porridge from the heat and cover to keep warm.

Preheat the oven to 425°F/220°C/gas 7.

Season the fillets on both sides with salt and pepper. In a large, ovenproof frying pan or Dutch oven, heat the remaining 2 tbsp olive oil over high heat. When the oil begins to shimmer, place the fillets in the pan, reduce the heat to medium, and cook until golden on the bottoms, about 3 minutes. Using a spatula, gently turn the fillets, taking care not to let them fall apart. Transfer the pan to the oven and bake until the fish is opaque throughout, about 3 minutes. Remove from the oven and add the remaining 2 tbsp butter to the pan alongside the fillets. As soon as the butter melts, use it to baste the tops of the fillets.

To serve, reheat the corn juice over medium heat, stirring, until warm. (If the juice seems too thick to spread easily, add 2 to 3 tbsp stock.) At the same time, reheat the corn porridge over medium heat, stirring frequently to prevent burning. Spread an oblong pool of the corn juice about 5 in/12 cm long and 3 in/7.5 cm wide in the center of each plate. Place two heaping spoonfuls of the corn porridge in the center of the pool of juice. Place a halibut fillet on top of the porridge. Serve at once.

baked salmon

with roasted beets and onion-clove purée

With pink salmon and crimson beets/beetroots topping a cream-colored purée, this colorful dish looks as good as it tastes. The buttery purée and sweet, smoky vegetables team up well with meaty salmon. Cippolini onions, smaller and sweeter than an average yellow onion, lend themselves well to sautéing. They offer a contrast in texture and color to the beets/beetroots. A hint of clove adds intrigue.

Any bright-edged sparkling or white wine will pair well here. But given the prevailing color scheme, a sparkling rosé or dry still rosé might be particularly apt.

4 red beets/beetroots, tops trimmed to 1 in/2.5 cm, scrubbed

4 golden beets/beetroots, tops trimmed to 1 in/2.5 cm, scrubbed

5 tbsp/70 g unsalted butter

3 large yellow onions, thinly sliced

½ cup/120 ml heavy (whipping)/ double cream

¼ tsp ground cloves

Salt

3 tbsp extra-virgin olive oil

3 bacon/streaky bacon slices, cut crosswise into matchsticks about ¼ in/6 mm thick

10 cippolini onions, peeled and quartered

¼ cup/60 ml Vegetable Stock (page 215) or canned low-sodium vegetable broth

Freshly ground pepper

4 salmon fillets, skin on, 5 to 6 oz/ 140 to 170 g each

Preheat the oven to 400°F/200°C/gas 6.

Place the beets/beetroots in a baking dish and cover them with a sheet of aluminum foil, crimping it loosely around the pan. Roast until tender and easily pierced with a fork, about 1 hour. Remove from the oven, take off the aluminum foil, and set aside until cool enough to handle. Peel the beets/beetroots using a carrot peeler or sharp paring knife. Cut into large (about ½ in/12 mm) dice, transfer to a bowl, and set aside.

In a large sauté pan or frying pan, melt 3 tbsp of the butter over medium heat. Add the yellow onions, raise the heat to medium-high, and stir to coat the onion slices with the butter. Cook, stirring frequently to prevent browning, until the onions are fully wilted and tender, about 30 minutes. Add the cream and cloves, reduce the heat to medium, and cook, stirring occasionally, for 5 minutes longer to allow the flavors to blend. Season with salt. Transfer the onion mixture to a blender or food processor and process to a smooth purée. Set aside.

CONTINUED

Preheat the oven again to 400°F/200°C/gas 6.

In another large sauté pan, heat 1 tbsp of the olive oil over medium heat. Add the bacon and sauté until crisp, about 3 minutes. Add the cippolini onions and sauté until soft, about 10 minutes. Add the beets/beetroots, stock, and the remaining 2 tbsp butter. Reduce the heat to medium-low, stir gently to incorporate the butter, and cook until most of the liquid has evaporated, about 15 minutes. Remove from the heat and cover to keep warm.

While the vegetables are simmering, lightly oil a baking dish with 1 tbsp of the remaining olive oil. Salt and pepper the salmon fillets and drizzle them with the last 1 tbsp olive oil. Place the fillets in the pan, skin-side down, and bake until opaque throughout, about 15 minutes.

Remove the salmon from the oven and set aside. In a saucepan, quickly reheat the onion-clove purée over medium heat. Spread a circle of the warm purée about 6 in/15 cm in diameter in the center of each plate. Arrange the vegetables on top of the purée, dividing them evenly. Arrange a salmon fillet on each plate, leaning it at an angle on the bed of vegetables. Serve at once.

baked swordfish
with green lentils and ginger aioli

Meaty swordfish and smoky lentils form a fine partnership, especially when topped with a high-toned ginger aioli. Look for firm, fresh steaks at the fish counter. And, if possible, use small, dark, blue-green French lentils (also referred to as du Puy lentils).

Consider any number of fine white wines as complements. For best results, the wines need a healthy dose of fruit flavor and acidity. Sparkling wine, Chardonnay, Riesling, Gewürztraminer, Viognier, and Roussanne would all add a special touch. Light, fruity reds like Pinot Noir and Grenache are also worth trying.

FOR THE GINGER AIOLI:

2 tsp Dijon mustard

1 large egg yolk, at room temperature

¼ cup/60 ml extra-virgin olive oil

¼ cup/60 ml canola oil

1 tbsp peeled and minced fresh ginger

Salt

2 bacon/streaky bacon slices, cut crosswise into matchsticks about ¼ in/6 mm thick

4 tbsp/60 ml extra-virgin olive oil

½ yellow onion, diced

3½ cups/840 ml Chicken Stock (page 216) or canned low-sodium chicken broth

1 cup French green lentils

2 garlic cloves, chopped

10 fresh thyme sprigs or 1 tsp dried thyme

10 black peppercorns

1 bay leaf

2 carrots, peeled and diced

4 swordfish steaks, 5 to 6 oz/140 to 170 g each

Salt and freshly ground pepper

TO MAKE THE AIOLI: In a medium bowl, combine the mustard and egg yolk. Very gradually add the oils in a fine, steady stream, whisking until they emulsify into a pale yellow, thick sauce. Whisk in the ginger. Season with salt. Cover and refrigerate for up to 24 hours.

In a large saucepan, sauté the bacon over medium heat just until it begins to turn golden, about 2½ minutes. Do not let it become crisp. Add 2 tbsp of the olive oil and the onion and sauté until the onion is translucent, about 3 minutes. Add the stock, raise the heat to high, and bring to a boil. Stir in the lentils and reduce the heat to maintain a simmer. Wrap the garlic, thyme, peppercorns, and bay leaf in cheesecloth/muslin and tie closed with twine to make a bouquet garni. Add the bouquet garni to the lentils and continue to simmer, uncovered, for 30 minutes.

Remove the bouquet garni and discard. Add the carrots and simmer until the lentils and carrots are tender, about 10 minutes. If any liquid remains, strain the lentils and discard the liquid, then return the lentils to the pan. Cover and set aside.

Preheat the oven to 450°F/230°C/gas 8.

Season the swordfish steaks on both sides with salt and pepper. In a large, ovenproof frying pan or Dutch oven, heat the remaining 2 tbsp olive oil over high heat. When the oil begins to shimmer, place the steaks in the pan, reduce the heat to medium-high, and sear until golden on the bottoms, about 2 minutes. Turn the steaks and transfer the pan to the oven. Bake until the fish is opaque throughout, about 5 minutes. Be careful not to overcook; the steaks should remain moist and soft inside.

Divide the lentils among warmed plates, mounding them in the center. Arrange a swordfish steak, golden-side up, on each plate, leaning it at an angle on the bed of lentils. Garnish each steak with a large dollop of the aioli and serve at once.

striped bass
with forbidden black rice and chorizo

This dish is quite easy to prepare but requires some attention when finishing off the fish and the rice simultaneously. Striped bass fillets are light and flaky when cooked properly, but they will fall apart and become mushy if overcooked. You can substitute any other light-textured fillet, such as rock cod or petrale sole.

According to legend, the medium-grain Chinese black rice once eaten exclusively by the emperors and related ruling classes was known as "forbidden" rice. You can find it in most Asian markets and specialty-food shops, but whole-grain brown rice makes a reasonable substitute (just remember that brown rice will take about 10 minutes longer to cook). Here, we spike the rice with spicy Spanish chorizo sausage.

A buttery, barrel-fermented Chardonnay would pair well here; so would a lighter-bodied Sauvignon Blanc, Chenin Blanc, or dry rosé.

1¾ cups/420 ml cold water

1 cup/215 g Chinese "forbidden" black rice

4 skinless striped bass fillets, about 5 oz/ 140 g each

Salt and freshly ground pepper

2 tbsp extra-virgin olive oil

½ cup/120 ml Chicken Stock (page 216) or canned low-sodium broth

4 oz/115 g chorizo, skin removed, cut into ¼-in/6-mm dice (about 1 cup)

4 tbsp/55 g unsalted butter

1 tbsp fresh lemon juice, plus 12 very thin lemon wedges and more juice for serving

2 tbsp minced fresh cilantro/fresh coriander

In a medium saucepan over high heat, bring the water to a boil. Add the rice, return to a boil, and reduce the heat to medium-low. Cover and cook until all of the liquid is absorbed, about 30 minutes. (The rice will not be fully cooked.) Remove from the heat and set aside, still covered.

Season the fillets on both sides with salt and pepper. In a large sauté pan or frying pan, heat the olive oil over medium-high heat until it shimmers. Place the fish fillets in the pan and reduce the heat to medium-low. Cook until the edges turn white, about 4 minutes.

While the fish is cooking, in a large saucepan, bring the stock to a boil over high heat. Add the chorizo, 2 tbsp of the butter, and the cooked rice. Reduce the heat to medium and stir the rice thoroughly. Simmer until the liquid is absorbed, about 3 minutes. Cover and set aside. (Be careful to monitor the progress of your fish, which will need to be flipped in the pan at about the same time.)

As the edges of the fish turn white, add the remaining 2 tbsp butter to the pan. Lift the pan slightly and tilt it back and forth to melt the butter. When the butter has melted, using a spatula, gently turn the fillets, taking care not to let them fall apart. Baste the fillets with the melted butter for about 20 seconds and continue to cook until opaque throughout, about 1 minute longer.

To serve, mound ½ to 1 cup/70 to 140 g rice in the center of each plate. Place a fish fillet on top of the rice. Add the 1 tbsp lemon juice to the pan and swirl it into the remaining melted butter and juices. Drizzle the lemon butter over each fillet and garnish with lemon wedges and cilantro/ fresh coriander. If you like, dot each serving with a little more lemon juice. Serve at once.

skate
with brown butter and sautéed new potatoes

Skate ply the Pacific coastal waters in profusion. The wings of this graceful swimmer are beautiful to behold, particularly as they fan out on your plate in a lovely white, ridged arch. In France, this classic dish is called *raie au beurre noir*. While the butter is not really "black," as the English translation would have us believe, it takes on a rich brown hue—and an exquisite, nutty, complex flavor—just before it starts to burn, which is why you need to be vigilant over the butter pan. Nevertheless, making a traditional brown butter sauce is as simple as melting butter.

The fish is mild flavored, with a delicate, meaty texture, and perfectly suited to its buttery dressing. Make sure you purchase wings that have been skinned and had the soft cartilage that runs through their center removed. Most fishmongers today do this automatically.

In your wineglass, a bright, fresh white varietal will best serve your needs—preferably one with limited or no oak influence. Think Sauvignon Blanc or unwooded Chardonnay.

1¼ lb/570 g new red potatoes, scrubbed but not peeled

Salt

6 tbsp/85 g unsalted butter

1 cup/240 ml dry white wine

1 bay leaf

4 skate wings, about 8 oz/225 g each, skin and cartilage removed by the fishmonger

4 tsp capers

1 lemon, cut into 4 wedges

4 tbsp/8 g minced fresh flat-leaf (Italian) parsley

Freshly ground pepper

Put the potatoes in a medium saucepan and add cold water to cover by 2 in/5 cm. Bring to a boil over high heat, stir in 1 tsp salt, and reduce the heat to maintain a simmer. Cook until the potatoes are tender and easily pierced with a fork, about 10 minutes. Drain in a colander and rinse under cold running water. When the potatoes are cool enough to handle, cut them in half.

In a large sauté pan or frying pan, melt 2 tbsp of the butter over medium-high heat. When the butter starts to bubble, place the potato halves in the pan, cut-side down. Sprinkle with ½ tsp salt and shake the pan gently to mix. Reduce the heat to medium-low and cook, gently stirring the potatoes or shaking the pan every 2 to 3 minutes, until the cut sides are golden brown, about 15 minutes. Remove from the heat and cover to keep warm.

Preheat the oven to 200°F/95°C.

In a large sauté pan or frying pan with deep sides, combine 6 cups/1.4 l water and the wine and bring to a boil over high heat. Add 1 tsp salt and the bay leaf. Place the skate wings in the water and cover the pan. Return to a simmer, then reduce the heat to medium and cook until the fish is tender and opaque throughout, about 5 minutes. Using a spatula, carefully transfer the wings to a large, ovenproof platter. (If the wings are too large to remove whole without breaking, cut them in half in the pan.) Drain any water that collects in the platter and place in the oven to keep the skate wings warm.

Reheat the potatoes over medium heat. While they are warming, in a small sauté pan, melt the remaining 4 tbsp butter over medium heat and cook until it foams and the surface turns dark brown. Watch carefully to prevent burning and remove from the heat as soon as most of the butter's surface is brown.

Divide the potatoes among warmed plates. Remove the skate wings from the oven and carefully place one on each plate next to the potatoes. Drizzle the brown butter over the skate and garnish each with 1 tsp of the capers and the juice of 1 lemon wedge. Sprinkle 1 tbsp of the parsley over the contents of each plate. Season with salt and pepper. Serve at once.

poultry and meats

While it's hard to say exactly why poultry and meats remain the centerpiece of so many great meals, perhaps we can explain it in part through the marriage of food and wine. At a very primary level, meat proteins bond naturally with tannins—the sometimes astringent structural components in most red wines—to soften texture and heighten fruitiness. The fats and oils in most meat and poultry dishes also benefit from both red and white wine's natural acidity, which provides balance and harmony on the palate.

From a more visceral perspective, a beautiful cut of meat or a plump, juicy roast bird evokes an appetizing anticipation that comes to most of us through our genetic heritage. The seductive smell of grilled meats on the barbecue probably has the same effect on our modern-day sensibilities as it did on our early ancestors long ago.

With this in mind, some of the preparations in this chapter might be considered particularly primal. Roasted Quail with Israeli Couscous, Black Mission Figs, and Bacon Vinaigrette offers a very simply roasted bird, but framed in the complex composed flavors of the couscous. The same holds true for Duck Breast with Turnip Purée, Caramelized Carrots, and Braised Leeks. By contrast, other recipes include a fine-tuned gravy, like the Meyer lemon sauce in Pork Loin Chops with Ricotta Gnocchi in Sage Butter or the red wine sauce in Beef Tenderloin with Red Wine Sauce, Truffled Mashed Potatoes, and Haricots Verts to highlight new dimensions in taste.

In addition to its French roots, the restaurant at Domaine Chandon has benefited from other immigrant culinary influences in Northern California. You will find them, for example, in the heady aromas issuing from Thai Chicken with Jasmine Rice.

Whether roasted, braised, or sautéed, the meats and poultry featured in this chapter will bring a smile to your lips as you taste traditions both old and new. As throughout the book, each recipe offers suggested wine pairings. For a more in-depth discussion on how food and wine work together, see "Pairing Food and Wine: Finding the Perfect Match" (page 39).

recipes

thai chicken
with jasmine rice

Before you tuck in, take a deep whiff of this highly aromatic dish. The scent of fresh cilantro/fresh corian-der is carried up in a steamy wave of garlic, lime, and jalapeño. Once in your mouth, the chicken and rice do not disappoint. They are brimming with *umami*—the exotic fifth element of Asian cooking—and your palate will be quickly seduced.

Look in the Asian foods section of your local grocery store for a number of ingredients commonly used in Thai cuisine and featured here. They include jasmine rice, a fragrant, medium-grain white rice; and fish sauce, a basic Thai condiment.

In your wineglass, try a fresh light, sparkling wine or an equally refreshing unwooded Chardonnay.

Salt and freshly ground pepper

2 whole boneless, skinless chicken breasts (about 1½ lb/680 g total weight), cut into 1-in/2.5-cm cubes

2 cups/430 g jasmine rice

3 tbsp fish sauce

2 tbsp brown sugar/demerara sugar

2 tbsp fresh lime juice

½ cup/120 ml soy sauce

2 tsp distilled white vinegar

2 tbsp canola oil

1 tbsp peeled and grated fresh ginger

3 garlic cloves, minced

1 jalapeño chile, seeded and minced

1 red bell pepper/capsicum, seeded and diced

2 tbsp minced fresh cilantro/fresh coriander

Lightly salt and pepper the chicken on all sides and set aside.

In a medium saucepan, bring 4 cups/960 ml water to a boil over high heat. Add the rice and stir briefly. Reduce the heat to medium-low, cover, and cook until the rice is tender and all of the water is absorbed, 15 to 20 minutes. Remove from the heat, cover, and set aside.

Meanwhile, in a medium bowl, whisk together 2 cups/480 ml water, the fish sauce, sugar, lime juice, soy sauce, and vinegar. Set aside.

In a large saucepan, heat the canola oil over medium-high heat. Add the ginger and garlic and sauté until fragrant, about 30 seconds. Reduce the heat to medium and add the jalapeño. Cook, stirring gently, until the chile is soft, about 1 minute. Add the bell pepper/capsicum and sauté for 1 minute. Stir in the fish sauce mixture and raise the heat to high. When bubbles begin to form at the liquid's edge, add the chicken and stir to mix well. Reduce the heat to medium and simmer until the chicken is opaque throughout, 12 to 15 minutes.

Use a fork to fluff the rice in the rice pot. To serve, divide the rice among 4 large, shallow bowls. Spoon the chicken with its sauce over the rice, garnish with cilantro/fresh coriander, and serve at once.

chicken breasts

with toasted seme di melone pasta and thyme infusion

This hearty dish is a cross between a stew and a soup. Visually, it's quite lovely to behold, with red tomatoes, green spinach, black olives, and white pearl onions supporting a beautifully browned chicken breast. Sometimes we serve this with a small, whole chicken breast, but it is more practical to slice the breast just prior to serving as described following. *Seme di melone* is a ricelike pasta similar to orzo (which can be used as a substitute). It takes on a smoky edge when toasted and marries well with the herbal broth in this preparation. Making this dish requires a number of cooking steps, but they are not difficult. Approach them separately in the order given for greatest ease in the kitchen.

Red or white wines will pair well here. Among the reds, try Pinot Noir, Pinot Meunier, Merlot, or Cabernet Franc. A white, grassy Sauvignon Blanc would also be excellent.

9 cups/2.25 l Chicken Stock (page 216) or canned low-sodium chicken broth

About 20 fresh thyme sprigs

1¼ cups/140 g dried *seme di melone* or orzo pasta

2 bacon/streaky bacon slices, diced

1 tbsp fresh lemon juice

2 celery stalks, trimmed and cut into slices ⅓ in/8 mm thick

15 pearl onions

4 tbsp/60 ml extra-virgin olive oil

10 cherry tomatoes, halved

⅓ cup/40 g Niçoise, Kalamata, or other small black olives, pitted and halved

3 tbsp finely chopped fresh chives

4 oz/115 g baby spinach leaves (about 3 cups firmly packed)

Salt and freshly ground pepper

2 boneless, skin-on chicken breast halves (about 1 lb/455 g total weight)

In a medium saucepan, combine 4 cups/960 ml of the stock and 10 of the thyme sprigs and bring to a boil over high heat. Reduce the heat to medium-low and maintain a gentle simmer until the liquid is reduced by half, about 25 minutes. Remove and discard the thyme. Cover the thyme infusion and set aside.

In a saucepan, bring another 4 cups/960 ml of the stock to a boil over high heat. Reduce the heat to medium and maintain at a simmer. While the stock is heating, in a large, dry pot, toast the pasta over medium heat, stirring constantly, until it turns reddish-gold and develops a nutty aroma, 2 to 4 minutes. (Watch closely to prevent it from burning.) Carefully pour the hot stock into the large pot with the pasta. Raise the heat to high and bring to a boil. Reduce the heat to medium and cook until the pasta is tender, about 10 minutes. Drain in a colander and rinse under cold running water. Set aside.

CONTINUED

In a small saucepan, cook the bacon over medium-high heat until crisp, 2 to 3 minutes. Add the remaining 1 cup/240 ml stock and 4 to 6 of the thyme sprigs. Bring to a boil over high heat, then reduce the heat to medium-low and simmer until the liquid has reduced by half, about 5 minutes. Add the lemon juice and celery and continue to simmer until the celery is tender and most of the liquid has evaporated, about 3 minutes longer. Remove from the heat, discard the thyme, and set aside.

Preheat the oven to 450°F/230°C/gas 8.

Using a paring knife, cut a small X in the root end of each pearl onion. In a medium saucepan, bring 2 cups/480 ml water to a boil over high heat. Drop the onions into the boiling water and cook for 1 minute. Drain in a colander and immediately rinse under cold running water to cool. When cool, gently squeeze the onions from their skins.

In a large sauté pan or frying pan, heat 2 tbsp of the olive oil over medium heat. Add the onions and sauté for 2 minutes. Add the tomatoes, olives, and chives and sauté until the tomatoes start to wilt, about 3 minutes longer. Add the spinach and the celery mixture and stir until the spinach starts to wilt, about 2 minutes. Add the pasta, 1 cup/170 g at a time, and stir to reheat gently and mix thoroughly with the vegetables. Season with salt and pepper. Remove from the heat, cover, and set aside.

Lightly salt and pepper the chicken breasts on both sides. In a large, ovenproof frying pan or Dutch oven, heat the remaining 2 tbsp olive oil over high heat until it starts to shimmer. Place the chicken breasts, skin-side down, in the pan. Reduce the heat to medium-high and sear until the skin is brown and crisp, about 5 minutes. Transfer the pan to the oven and bake until the chicken is opaque throughout, about 15 minutes. Remove from the oven, transfer the breasts to a carving board, and let rest for about 3 minutes. Carve the chicken breasts crosswise into slices about 1 in/2.5 cm thick.

To serve, reheat the thyme infusion over medium heat until very hot but not boiling. Reheat the pasta and vegetable mixture gently over medium-low heat, stirring to prevent sticking or burning. Divide the pasta and vegetables among 4 large, shallow bowls. Place 3 or 4 slices of chicken on top of each serving. Carefully pour ½ cup/120 ml of the hot thyme broth over the contents of each bowl. Garnish each with a thyme sprig and serve at once.

roasted quail
with israeli couscous, black mission figs, and bacon vinaigrette

In this colorful dish, crisp, browned quail sit atop pasta flecked with green wilted arugula/rocket, copper-colored bacon bits, and dark figs—all garnished with bright orange zest. The smoky bacon, sweet dried fruit, and tangy zest serve well as a backdrop for these small, meaty birds.

Israeli couscous, sometimes referred to as pearl couscous, bears little resemblance to traditional yellow, tiny-grained North African couscous. The Israeli version is a pasta with larger white grains that look like barley or small peas. It has a creamy-soft mouth-feel and a nutty flavor. It's also quite easy to cook. This dish is also delicious when prepared with lentils, particularly the green French du Puy variety. Note that lentils, unlike the couscous below, should not be browned prior to cooking. Lentils also require a longer cooking time, 30 to 40 minutes.

Aside from marinating the quail, this entire recipe can be prepared in under an hour. The birds are best when marinated at least 4 hours in advance, and preferably overnight. However, if you run out of time or just forget to plan in advance, a shorter marinating time will still yield reasonably good results.

The bold flavors in this recipe cry out for similarly fruity, bold flavors in red wines such as Zinfandel, Petite Sirah, and Syrah. In addition, the pretty cherry qualities found in Pinot Noir and Pinot Meunier would make them fine pairing candidates. Or try a fruity, dry rosé.

4 quail, boned

9 tbsp/135 ml extra-virgin olive oil

4 garlic cloves, coarsely chopped

1 tbsp dried thyme, plus 1 tsp

1 cup/115 g pearl onions

1 cup/115 g Israeli (pearl) couscous

Salt

2 cups/480 ml boiling water

6 to 8 dried or fresh black mission figs, stemmed and quartered

3 bacon/streaky bacon slices, cut crosswise into matchsticks about ¼ in/6 mm thick

1 large egg yolk

1 tsp sherry vinegar

1 tsp honey

1 tbsp Dijon mustard

2 cups/55 g arugula/rocket, tough stems removed

Freshly ground pepper

Zest of 1 orange

In a zippered plastic bag or plastic container with a tight-fitting lid, combine the quail, 4 tbsp/ 60 ml of the olive oil, the garlic, and the 1 tbsp thyme and turn the birds to coat thoroughly with the marinade. Seal the bag or container and let marinate in the refrigerator for at least 4 hours and up to overnight.

CONTINUED

Preheat the oven to 400°F/200°C/gas 6.

Using a paring knife, cut a small X in the root end of each pearl onion. In a saucepan, bring 2 cups/480 ml water to a boil over high heat. Plunge the onions into the boiling water and cook for 1 minute. Drain in a colander and immediately rinse under cold running water to cool. When cool, gently squeeze the onions from their skins. Set aside.

In a medium saucepan, heat 1 tbsp of the olive oil over medium heat. Add the couscous and sauté until about half of the grains are lightly browned, about 5 minutes. Add a pinch of salt and the boiling water. Return the water to a boil, reduce the heat to low, cover, and simmer until all the liquid has been absorbed, 10 to 12 minutes. Remove from the heat. Uncover, place the figs on top of the hot couscous, re-cover the pan, and set aside.

In a large frying pan, cook the bacon over medium-high heat until crisp, about 3 minutes. Remove the bacon bits with a slotted spoon and reserve. Pour the hot bacon grease from the pan into a small bowl and reserve. Return the same pan (without cleaning it) to the stovetop over medium-low heat. Add 1 tbsp of the olive oil and the onions. Sauté until the onions are lightly browned on all sides, about 10 minutes.

While the onions are cooking, make the bacon vinaigrette. In a small bowl, combine the egg yolk, vinegar, honey, mustard, 1 tbsp of the olive oil, the reserved bacon grease, and the 1 tsp dried thyme. Whisk together until thickened and emulsified and set aside.

When the onions are browned, add 2 tbsp water to the pan and use a wooden spoon to scrape up any browned bits from the bottom of the pan. Add the couscous and figs. Fold in the bacon vinaigrette, the reserved bacon bits, and the arugula/rocket and stir gently until the arugula has wilted and all the ingredients are well blended. Remove from the heat. Season with salt and pepper, cover, and set aside.

Remove the quail from the marinade and sprinkle lightly with salt and pepper. In a large, oven-proof frying pan or Dutch oven, heat the remaining 2 tbsp olive oil over medium-high heat. When the oil begins to shimmer, place the quail in the pan, breast-side down, and sear until lightly browned, 2 to 3 minutes. Transfer the pan to the oven and roast until the birds lose their translucent, milky color on top, 12 to 15 minutes.

Divide the couscous mixture among warmed plates, mounding it in the center. (The couscous will be warm. If you want it hotter, reheat it on the stovetop for a minute or so prior to serving.) Arrange a quail, breast-side up, on each plate, leaning it at an angle against the bed of couscous. Garnish the contents of the plates with salt and freshly ground pepper and the orange zest. Serve at once.

duck breast

with turnip purée, caramelized carrots, and braised leeks

In this recipe, meaty duck breast is flanked by two fabulous sides: a wonderfully light-textured, turnip purée topped with sweet, buttery carrots, and lemony leeks that balance the rich, savory bird. For best results, prepare this dish in the order it is presented, prepping all ingredients in advance. It's easy to reheat the purée and carrots prior to serving.

Duck is particularly wine friendly. Fruit-driven, elegant red wines such as Pinot Noir and Pinot Meunier would work well in your glass. We also recommend a lush, buttery Chardonnay, or fruity Riesling or Gewürztraminer among whites.

3 large turnips (about 1½ lb/680 g total weight), peeled and diced

1½ cups/360 ml heavy (whipping)/ double cream

4 tbsp/85 g unsalted butter

Salt

2 large carrots, peeled and cut into thin rounds

4 medium leeks

2 boneless duck breasts, about 1 lb/455 g each

Freshly ground pepper

1 tbsp canola oil

Fresh lemon juice for serving

In a saucepan over medium-high heat, combine the turnips, cream, and 1 tbsp of the butter. Add a pinch of salt and bring to a simmer. Reduce the heat to medium and continue to simmer until the turnips are tender, about 15 minutes. Transfer the turnip mixture to a blender or food processor and, working in batches if necessary, process to a smooth purée. Taste and adjust the seasoning with salt. Transfer the purée to a large bowl, cover, and set aside.

In a small sauté pan or frying pan, melt 1 tbsp of the butter over medium heat. Reduce the heat to low, add the carrots, and sauté until tender and golden brown, about 10 minutes. Season with salt. Remove from the heat and set aside.

In a medium sauté pan or frying pan, melt 2 tbsp of the butter over medium heat. Add the leeks and sauté, turning occasionally to avoid burning, about 4 minutes. Add ½ cup/120 ml water, bring to a boil over high heat, then reduce the heat to maintain a gentle simmer. Cover and cook until the leeks are tender, about 15 minutes. Uncover the pan and continue to braise until most, but not all, of the liquid has evaporated. Remove from the heat, re-cover, and set aside.

Cut each duck breast in half lengthwise and trim away excess fat. (Do not remove the skin.) Using a fork, poke 4 or 5 evenly spaced holes in the skin of each breast. (This will allow the rendered fat to drain into the pan.) Lightly salt and pepper the duck breasts on both sides.

CONTINUED

In a large frying pan or sauté pan, heat the canola oil over medium-high heat. Place the breasts, skin-side down, in the pan and cook until the skin is crisp, 6 to 8 minutes. Spoon off and discard the rendered fat from the pan. Reduce the heat to medium, turn the breasts, and cook for 3 to 4 minutes longer for medium-rare. Transfer the breasts to a carving board and let rest for 5 minutes.

While the meat is resting, return the turnip purée to a saucepan and reheat over medium heat, stirring occasionally. (You can also reheat in a microwave oven.) Reheat the carrots over medium heat, stirring gently. Carve the duck breasts crosswise into slices about ¼ in/6 mm thick.

Fan 4 or 5 slices of duck in the center of each of 4 warmed plates. Place a leek to one side of the duck breast slices and cut it in half lengthwise. Sprinkle each leek with a few drops—no more than ¼ tsp—of lemon juice. On the other side of the duck breast, mound the turnip purée, dividing it evenly. Top each mound of turnip purée with 1 tbsp of the caramelized carrots. Alternatively, fan the duck slices on top of the turnip puree. Garnish the duck, leek, and purée with a generous amount of freshly ground pepper. Serve at once.

braised rabbit
with fava beans, celery root, and orange zest

The slow-cooked meat in this hearty stew is so tender, it literally falls off the bone. Rabbit, on its own, is quite mild-mannered. But here, it takes on the rich flavors of its orange-infused sauce with gusto. Celery root and fresh fava/broad beans provide a wonderfully light contrast on the side.

Cutting a rabbit into pieces prior to cooking isn't much different than cutting a chicken. But if your rabbit doesn't come precut at the store, it's easiest to have your butcher do it for you.

As a beverage accompaniment, red wine is de rigueur—and the choices are legion. Lighter reds, such as Pinot Noir and Sangiovese would make excellent pairings. So would more robust Merlot, Cabernet Sauvignon, and Syrah.

Salt and freshly ground pepper

1 rabbit (about 3 lb/1.4 kg), cut into 6 pieces, including legs and thighs

5 tbsp/75 ml extra-virgin olive oil

½ cup/120 ml Veal Demi-Glace (page 217 or store-bought)

6 garlic cloves, minced

10 cippolini onions

2 leeks, white parts only, cut into rounds ¼ in/6 mm thick

2 carrots, peeled and cut into 1-in/2.5-cm rounds

5 fresh thyme sprigs

3 large pieces orange zest, 5 to 6 in/12 to 15 cm long and ¼ to ½ in/6 to 12 mm wide

3 cups/720 ml dry red wine

½ cup/120 ml fresh orange juice

3 lb/1.4 kg fresh, unshelled fava/broad beans

1 large celery root (about 1¾ lb/800 g), peeled and cut into 1-in/2.5-cm cubes

½ cup/120 ml Chicken Stock (page 216) or canned low-sodium chicken broth

Preheat the oven to 325°F/165°C/gas 3.

Lightly salt and pepper the rabbit pieces on all sides. In a Dutch oven or large, ovenproof saucepan with a lid, heat 2 tbsp of the olive oil over medium-high heat. Add the rabbit pieces and sear, turning occasionally, until golden brown on all sides, 4 to 5 minutes. Remove from the heat and transfer the rabbit pieces to a plate. Reserve the pot on the stovetop.

In a small saucepan, bring 2 cups/480 ml water to a boil over high heat. Add the demi-glace and stir to dissolve. Remove from the heat and set aside.

Add 1 tbsp of the olive oil to the pot you used to sear the rabbit and heat over medium heat. Add half of the garlic and sauté until fragrant, about 30 seconds. Add the onions and leeks, stir to mix well, and sauté until the leeks have wilted, about 3 minutes. Add the carrots, thyme, and orange zest. Sauté until the carrots begin to soften, about 2 minutes longer.

Add the wine, orange juice, demi-glace, 1 tsp salt, and pepper to taste and stir to mix thoroughly. Raise the heat to high and bring to a boil. Remove from the heat and return the rabbit to the pot, nestling the pieces into the liquid. Cover the pot and transfer to the oven. Braise for 1½ hours. Uncover and continue to braise until the liquid has reduced by about one-third its volume, about 30 minutes longer. Remove from the oven, re-cover to keep warm, and set aside until ready to serve.

As the rabbit nears being done, prepare the fava/broad beans and celery root. Remove the beans from their pods. In a medium saucepan, bring 3 in/7.5 cm salted water to a boil over high heat. Add the beans and cook for 2 minutes. Drain in a colander and rinse under cold running water to cool. Using your thumb and forefinger, pinch off and discard the beans' outer skins. Set the peeled beans aside.

Put the celery root in another medium saucepan and add water to cover by 2 in/5 cm. Stir in a large pinch of salt. Bring to a boil over high heat, then reduce the heat to medium and cook until tender but still firm to the bite, 5 to 7 minutes. Drain in a colander and rinse under cold running water to halt the cooking. Set aside.

In a medium saucepan, heat the remaining 2 tbsp olive oil over medium heat. Add the remaining garlic and sauté until fragrant, about 30 seconds. Add the fava/broad beans and celery root and stir to coat evenly with the olive oil and garlic. Add the chicken stock, raise the heat to high, and bring to a boil. Reduce the heat to low, cover, and simmer until the beans and celery root are tender, about 10 minutes. Uncover and continue to simmer until most of the liquid has evaporated, 5 to 10 minutes longer. Taste and adjust the seasoning.

Remove and discard the thyme sprigs and orange zest from the rabbit pot. (The rabbit should still be quite warm. If not, reheat gently over medium heat.) Spoon the braised rabbit and its thick sauce and vegetables onto warmed plates, arranging it on one side of the plates. Arrange the bean and celery root mixture on the opposite side of the plates for a pleasing color contrast. Serve at once.

pork loin chops
with ricotta gnocchi in sage butter

These tender pork loin chops are topped with a rich, tangy sauce that gets its verve from Meyer lemons, which are milder than conventional lemons. Meyers are believed to be derived from a cross between a lemon and an orange. They are not as available year-round as traditional lemons, which are equally suitable for this dish. And if you don't have a stash of homemade veal stock handy, buy a small container of commercial demi-glace, which can be easily transformed into the rich stock used to make the sauce.

However, the star of this show just might be the ricotta gnocchi. Typically, gnocchi are made with potatoes. This version, made with ricotta cheese and flour, is lighter and fluffier than its potato-based cousin. Creamy-smooth on the inside and coated with a fresh sage–infused butter sauce, these gnocchi are so good, you could confidently feature them as a main course on their own.

This is the kind of dish that marries well with many kinds of wines, both red and white. Rich, barrel-fermented Chardonnay, or fruity Riesling, Gewürztraminer, and Viognier would all complement the meat and the buttery gnocchi. Lighter, fruity reds with good acidity, such as Pinot Noir or Zinfandel, would also play well here.

FOR THE GNOCCHI:

1 lb/455 g whole-milk ricotta cheese

2 large eggs, lightly beaten

¼ cup/30 g freshly grated Romano cheese

2 cups/260 g all-purpose/plain flour, plus more for dusting

1 tsp salt

1 cup/240 ml Veal Stock (page 217 or made from a store-bought demi-glace)

2 tbsp fresh Meyer lemon juice

1 tbsp sugar

Salt

Freshly ground pepper

4 pork loin chops, 6 to 8 oz/170 to 225 g each

2 tbsp extra-virgin olive oil

½ cup/115 g unsalted butter, cut into 6 large pieces

¼ cup/7 g chopped fresh sage

TO MAKE THE GNOCCHI: In a large bowl, combine the ricotta, eggs, Romano, 1 cup/130 g of the flour, and the salt. Using a wooden spoon, stir vigorously to blend well. The mixture should be light and fluffy. Refrigerate the ricotta mixture for at least 30 minutes and up to 1 hour to allow it to firm up.

While the ricotta mixture is resting, in a small saucepan over medium-high heat, combine the stock, lemon juice, and sugar and stir to mix well. Bring to a boil, then reduce the heat to low and simmer, stirring occasionally, until the liquid has reduced and thickened into a rich sauce, about 5 minutes. Taste and adjust the seasoning with salt. Remove the lemon sauce from the heat and set aside.

CONTINUED

Pour the remaining 1 cup/130 g flour onto a clean work surface. Using a large spoon, scoop out four equal portions of the ricotta mixture onto the floured surface. Dust your hands with flour, take up one scoop of the ricotta mixture, and roll in the flour, kneading lightly until you incorporate enough flour to form a soft dough. Dust your hands and the work surface with more flour as needed to prevent sticking. Repeat with the remaining portions of ricotta mixture. Using only your hands, shape each dough piece into a rope ½ to ¾ in/12 mm to 2 cm in diameter and about 12 in/30.5 cm long. Cut each rope crosswise into nuggets (or little pillows) about 1 in/2.5 cm long. Gently roll each piece lightly in more flour to shape and prevent sticking. You will produce about 50 gnocchi.

Bring a large pot three-fourths full of lightly salted water to a boil. Have ready a large bowl of ice water and a baking sheet/tray lined with parchment/baking paper.

Using a slotted spoon, carefully place 15 to 20 gnocchi in the boiling water. When the gnocchi float to the surface, 1 to 2 minutes, use the slotted spoon to transfer them to the ice bath. (The cooling firms them up and makes them easier to sauté in the final step.) When the gnocchi are cool, using the slotted spoon, transfer them to the paper. Repeat to cook the remaining gnocchi. Set aside.

Position a rack in the lower third of the oven and preheat to 450°F/230°C/gas 8.

Lightly salt and pepper the pork chops on both sides. In a Dutch oven or large, ovenproof frying pan, heat the olive oil over high heat. When the oil starts to shimmer, place the chops in the pan and sear until golden brown, about 2 minutes per side. Transfer the pot to the lower rack of the oven and bake until an instant-read thermometer inserted into the thickest part of a chop registers 150°F/65°C, 8 to 10 minutes.

Immediately after placing the meat in the oven, in a large sauté pan or frying pan over medium-high heat, melt the butter. (The pan should be large enough to fit all the gnocchi in a single layer. If you don't have a pan large enough, divide the butter, gnocchi, and sage between two pans.) When the butter has melted, reduce the heat to medium and gently stir in the sage with a wooden spoon. Add the gnocchi and sauté until browned on the first side, 2 to 3 minutes. Using a spatula or slotted spoon, carefully turn the gnocchi and sauté until browned on the second side, about 2 minutes longer. Remove from the heat.

When the gnocchi are almost done, the loin chops will also be done or almost done. Reheat the lemon sauce over medium-low heat. As soon as the chops are done, remove from the oven and let rest in the pan for 2 to 3 minutes.

Place a loin chop on each plate and garnish each with 1 to 2 tbsp lemon sauce. Arrange 10 to 12 sage butter–drenched gnocchi beside each chop. Serve at once.

braised short ribs
with creamy polenta

This dish may be the very definition of comfort food. The tender, flavorful, slow-cooked meat rests upon a creamy-soft bed of polenta—all so satisfying on a very basic level. Fresh peas and cippolini onions enhance the dish. Small, flat cippolinis are sweet onions that are fairly easy to find in most supermarkets. If they're not available, you can substitute smaller pearl onions; you'll need about twice as many.

Note that the recipe calls for a full bottle of red wine. The finer qualities of what we love to drink in a wine are almost entirely lost in the cooking process, so we recommend using any drinkable but inexpensive red wine for the pot. (For more information about cooking with wine, see page 46.) Save your better wines for your glass—these ribs call out for a hearty Syrah or a full-bodied Cabernet Sauvignon.

Salt and freshly ground pepper

4 to 6 bone-in short ribs (about 2 lb/910 g total weight)

1 large yellow onion, cut into large cubes

2 leeks, white parts only, cut into rounds 1 in/2.5 cm thick and rinsed and drained thoroughly

2 carrots, peeled and cut into 1-in/2.5-cm chunks

5 garlic cloves, halved

1 bottle (750 ml) dry red wine

4 tbsp/60 ml extra-virgin olive oil

6 to 8 fresh thyme sprigs

1 bay leaf

1½ lb/680 g fresh peas, shelled (about 1½ cups/215 g)

8 cippolini onions, peeled and quartered

¼ cup/60 ml Vegetable Stock (page 215) or canned low-sodium vegetable broth

1 tbsp unsalted butter

FOR THE POLENTA:

1 cup/240 ml heavy (whipping)/ double cream

Salt

1 cup/140 g yellow polenta

2 tbsp unsalted butter

½ cup/60 g freshly grated Parmesan cheese

Freshly ground pepper

Lightly salt and pepper the ribs on all sides. In a large, nonreactive bowl, combine the ribs, yellow onion, leeks, carrots, garlic, and 2 cups/480 ml of the red wine. Cover and let marinate in the refrigerator overnight or for up to 24 hours.

Preheat the oven to 350°F/180°C/gas 4.

In a Dutch oven or large, ovenproof saucepan with a lid, heat 3 tbsp of the olive oil over medium-high heat. Remove the ribs from the marinade (reserve the marinade) and sear the ribs until dark brown on all sides, about 2 minutes per side. Transfer the ribs to a plate. Reduce the heat to medium and, using a slotted spoon, add the vegetables from the marinade to the pot. Sauté, stirring occasionally, until soft, about 10 minutes.

CONTINUED

Add the wine from the marinade plus the remaining red wine in the bottle to the pot. Stir in the thyme, bay leaf, and ½ tsp salt. Raise the heat to high and bring to a boil. Remove from the heat. Return the ribs and any juices accumulated on the plate to the pot, cover, and transfer to the oven. Braise for 2 hours, stirring every 30 to 40 minutes.

Remove the pot from the oven and uncover. The meat should be very tender, and some may be falling off the bone. The sauce will be thick, but if you'd like a thicker consistency, simmer over low heat, uncovered, for about 10 minutes. Remove and discard the bay leaf and thyme sprigs. Re-cover to keep warm and set aside until ready to serve.

Bring a small pot half full of lightly salted water to a boil over high heat. Add the peas and cook until tender but still slightly crunchy, about 3 minutes. Drain in a colander and rinse with ice-cold water. Return the peas to the pot and set aside.

In a medium sauté pan or frying pan, heat the remaining 1 tbsp olive oil over medium heat. Add the cippolini onions and sauté until translucent, about 5 minutes. Add the stock, bring to a simmer, and cook until the stock is reduced by one-fourth, about 3 minutes. Remove from the heat and set aside.

TO MAKE THE POLENTA: In a medium saucepan over high heat, combine 4 cups/960 ml water, the cream, and 1 tsp salt and bring to a boil. Reduce the heat to medium and slowly pour the polenta into the pot in a stream, stirring with a whisk. Using a wooden spoon, stir the polenta frequently—about every 45 seconds—until it has thickened to a rich, creamy texture, 8 to 10 minutes. Remove from the heat. Add the 2 tbsp butter and the Parmesan and stir to mix well. Taste and adjust the seasoning with salt and pepper.

Add the peas to the onions and reheat over medium-low heat, stirring in the 1 tbsp butter until it melts. (The ribs should still be quite warm. If not, reheat gently over medium heat.) Spoon a large serving of polenta in a circle on each dinner plate. Arrange the sauce and vegetables from the braising pot in the center of the polenta. Top with the peas and onions. Place 1 or 2 short ribs on top of the polenta, sauce, and all of the vegetables. Serve at once.

beef tenderloin
with red wine sauce, truffled mashed potatoes, and haricots verts

True to its name, beef tenderloin is possibly the most tender, buttery-textured cut of meat you will ever eat. It is accompanied here with earthy, truffled mashed potatoes and the French-style string beans called haricots verts—typically more slender than your average American string bean. If you can't find haricots verts, any green string beans will do. Truffle butter and truffle oil can be found in most specialty-food shops. They're not inexpensive, but they are far less costly than whole truffles. Look for a small (3-oz/85-g) container of the butter and a modest (3- to 4-oz/85- to 115-g) bottle of the infused oil to keep your budget in check.

None of the techniques used here are particularly complicated, but timing is important for ease of preparation. Marinate the meat overnight—or for at least 8 hours—prior to cooking. When it's time to use the stove, make the potatoes first and reheat them on the stovetop or in a microwave immediately before serving. For the phase when it all comes together, you will have to share your attention between roasting the meat, simmering the wine sauce, and sautéing the haricots verts, all of which require about the same amount of time on or in the stove. To make the steps of this deliciously rewarding dance simple and elegant, prep all of your ingredients in advance and have them laid out at the ready.

The recipe calls for six steaks to serve six people. For four diners, use four steaks but don't change any other ingredient quantities. You'll just have some potatoes and string beans as leftovers.

Red wine really does go well with red meat. These steaks aren't cheap. So choose a really good red wine—it doesn't matter what varietal—to make your meal most memorable.

Salt and freshly ground pepper

4 to 6 beef tenderloin steaks, about 6 oz/ 170 g each

1 tbsp dried thyme

6 garlic cloves, 3 thinly sliced and 3 minced

4 tbsp/60 ml extra-virgin olive oil, plus extra for drizzling

2½ lb/1.2 kg new white potatoes, peeled and cut into quarters

1 cup/240 ml half-and-half/half cream

3 oz/85 g purchased black truffle butter

1 cup/240 ml dry red wine

4 tbsp/55 g unsalted butter, cut into 4 pieces

1 lb/455 g French haricots verts or string beans, trimmed

Truffle oil for drizzling, or shaved fresh truffles for garnish (optional)

Lightly salt and pepper the steaks on both sides and sprinkle them with the thyme. Sprinkle the garlic slices on top of the steaks, dividing them evenly, and drizzle each with enough olive oil to moisten. Place the steaks on a platter and cover with plastic wrap/cling film (it's all right to stack the steaks on top of each other for a better fit on the platter). Refrigerate for at least 8 hours or up to 24 hours.

In a large saucepan, combine the potatoes with cold water to cover and bring to a boil over high heat. Reduce the heat to medium and cook until tender, 10 to 12 minutes.

CONTINUED

Drain the potatoes in a colander and return them to the pan. Add the half-and-half/half cream and use a hand-held potato masher to mash. Stir in the truffle butter and ½ tsp salt and continue to mash until the texture is fairly smooth. (Don't worry if your potatoes are slightly lumpy.) Taste and adjust the seasoning with salt and pepper. Cover to keep warm and set aside.

Preheat the oven to 475°F/240°C/gas 9. Place a rack in a large roasting pan/tray.

In a large sauté pan or frying pan, heat 2 tbsp of the olive oil over high heat. Unwrap the steaks and discard the garlic. When the oil starts to shimmer, place the steaks in the pan and sear for 2 minutes on each side. Transfer the steaks to the rack in the roasting pan. Roast until an instant-read thermometer inserted into the thickest part of a steak registers 135°F/57°C for medium-rare, 10 to 12 minutes.

While the meat is roasting, return the pan used for searing the meat to high heat. Add the wine and use a wooden spoon to scrape up any browned bits from the bottom of the pan. Bring to a boil, reduce the heat to medium-high, and simmer until the wine is reduced by two-thirds, 5 to 7 minutes. Add the unsalted butter and let it melt into the wine, stirring occasionally. Stir in ½ tsp salt and remove from the heat.

While the sauce is simmering and the meat is still in the oven, make the haricots verts. In a large sauté pan, heat the remaining 2 tbsp olive oil over medium heat. Add the minced garlic and sauté until fragrant but not browned, about 30 seconds. Add the beans and toss gently to coat evenly with the garlic and oil. Add 3 tbsp water, reduce the heat to low, cover, and simmer, stirring occasionally, until the beans are tender, about 10 minutes. If the liquid evaporates, add more water, 1 or 2 tbsp at a time, to keep the beans moist and prevent burning. Season with salt and pepper.

Gently reheat the potatoes and/or wine sauce, if necessary. Place a steak in the center of each warmed plate. Place a large scoop of truffled potatoes on one side of the steak and arrange a portion of haricot verts on the side opposite the steak. Drizzle truffle oil over the potatoes and drizzle the wine sauce on the plate. Add the shaved truffles over each steak, if desired. Serve at once.

veal chop roast

with horseradish jus and potato–wild mushroom hash

Meat and potatoes never tasted this good. Wild mushrooms and rendered duck fat—which you can find at most specialty-food stores—might have something to do with it. The rich *jus,* or gravy, offers very subtle hints of horseradish and thyme and dresses the tender veal to perfection.

If no wild mushrooms are available, commercial mushrooms such as button or cremini/brown are fine options. They may not provide the same excitement on the palate, but they still have a good rich and earthy taste.

You can't go wrong drinking red wine with this dish. Any varietal will work its own particular magic.

¼ cup/35 g grated fresh horseradish

1 tsp sugar

1 tsp rice wine vinegar

3 Yukon gold potatoes, peeled and cut into 1-in/2.5-cm cubes

Salt and freshly ground pepper

3½ lb/1.6 kg veal chop roast (with 4 or 5 chops), fat trimmed

2 tbsp extra-virgin olive oil

¼ cup/60 ml Veal Demi-Glace (page 217 or store-bought)

1 cup/240 ml very hot water

½ cup/120 ml dry red wine

2 tsp minced fresh thyme

¼ cup/60 ml rendered duck fat

1 leek, white part only, cut into rounds ¼ in/6 mm thick

1 lb/455 g mixed wild mushrooms such as porcini, shiitake, and chanterelle, brushed clean and thinly sliced

2 tbsp unsalted butter

In a small, nonreactive bowl, combine the horseradish, sugar, and vinegar. Stir well and set aside to marinate for 1 hour. Meanwhile, in a large saucepan, combine the potatoes and cold water to cover by 2 in/5 cm. Bring to a boil over high heat and cook until the potatoes are tender, 10 to 12 minutes. Drain in a colander and rinse under cold running water. Set aside.

Preheat the oven to 375°F/190°C/gas 5.

Lightly salt and pepper the veal roast on both sides. In a Dutch oven or other large, oven-proof saucepan, heat 1 tbsp of the olive oil over high heat and sear the roast, meat-side down, until nicely browned, about 5 minutes. Turn the roast bone-side down and transfer the pan to the oven. Roast until an instant-read thermometer inserted into the thickest part of the meat reaches 145°F/63°C, about 1 hour.

CONTINUED

While the meat is roasting, in a medium saucepan, whisk together the demi-glace and hot water. Add the red wine, the horseradish mixture, and the thyme and whisk thoroughly. Bring to a boil over high heat, then reduce the heat to medium-low. Simmer until the sauce thickens, 10 to 12 minutes. Drain through a fine-mesh sieve and return the liquid to the saucepan. Discard the solids. Set the horseradish *jus* aside.

In a large sauté pan, heat the duck fat over medium-high heat and add the potatoes. Cook until the bottoms are golden brown, 6 to 8 minutes. Using a spatula, turn the potatoes and sauté until golden on the second side, about 5 minutes longer. (Shake the pan occasionally to keep the potatoes from sticking.) Reserving the pan on the stovetop, transfer the potatoes to paper towels/absorbent papers to drain. Season with salt and set aside.

Add the remaining 1 tbsp olive oil to the duck fat to coat the saucepan and heat over medium heat. Add the leek and sauté until wilted, about 3 minutes. Stir in the mushrooms and sauté, shaking the pan or stirring occasionally to prevent sticking or burning, until they release their liquid and the leek and mushrooms are tender, about 10 minutes. Remove from the heat and set aside.

When the veal is done, transfer to a carving board, tent loosely with aluminum foil, and let rest for about 5 minutes. Place the roasting pan on the stovetop over medium-high heat and pour the horseradish *jus* into the pan. When it starts to bubble, reduce the heat to low, add 1 tbsp of the butter, and stir to mix well. Simmer, stirring occasionally, until thickened, about 5 minutes.

Reheat the mushrooms gently over medium heat. Add the remaining 1 tbsp butter and mix well as it melts. Add the potatoes and stir gently to mix all the ingredients while reheating, about 5 minutes.

Slice the veal roast into 4 chops, starting at the meaty end and cutting alongside the bone. Place 1 veal chop on each plate with a healthy serving of the potato and mushroom hash alongside it. Drizzle the horseradish *jus* on and around the veal chop. Serve at once.

braised veal cheeks
with celery root purée

These tender veal cheeks will practically melt in your mouth. They are easy to prepare and, once in the oven, pretty much take care of themselves. An added benefit is that they are well suited to entertaining late-arriving guests. Once the meat and the purée have cooked, they can be kept covered at room temperature for up to an hour or so if necessary. Just quickly reheat them on the stovetop or in a microwave prior to serving.

Celery root purée may look like mashed potatoes, but it is lighter in texture and has a distinctive, yet subtle, herbal taste. The light-bodied purée and the rich veal cheeks provide a nice contrast. They will be best appreciated alongside a bold red wine such as Cabernet Sauvignon, Merlot, or Syrah.

1 yellow onion, coarsely chopped

3 carrots, peeled and cut into 1-in/2.5-cm chunks

2 leeks, white parts only, cut into rounds ¼ in/6 mm thick and rinsed and drained thoroughly

10 fresh thyme sprigs

1 bottle (750 ml) dry red wine

4 veal cheeks (about 2 lb/910 kg total weight)

Salt and freshly ground pepper

2 tbsp extra-virgin olive oil

2 cups/480 ml Veal Stock (page 217 or made from a store-bought demi-glace)

2 celery roots (about 3 lb/1.4 kg total weight), peeled and cut into 2-in/5-cm cubes

2 tbsp unsalted butter

1 cup/240 ml heavy (whipping)/double cream

¼ cup/7 g minced fresh flat-leaf (Italian) parsley

In a large zippered plastic bag or plastic container with a tight-fitting lid, combine the onion, carrots, leeks, thyme, red wine, and veal cheeks. Seal the bag or container and let marinate in the refrigerator overnight or for up to 24 hours.

Preheat the oven to 325°F/165°C/gas 3.

Remove the veal cheeks from the marinade and pat dry with paper towels/absorbent papers. (Reserve the marinade.) Sprinkle with salt and pepper. In a Dutch oven or large, ovenproof saucepan with a lid, heat the olive oil over medium-high heat. When it starts to shimmer, sear the veal cheeks on each side until golden brown on both sides, about 2 minutes per side. Transfer the meat to a plate and set aside.

Add the liquid from the marinade to the pot and return to medium-high heat. Use a wooden spoon to scrape up any browned bits from the bottom of the pan. Bring to a boil and simmer for about 3 minutes. Add the stock and return to a boil, then reduce the heat and simmer for about 2 minutes longer. Add the vegetables from the marinade and return to a boil. Return the veal cheeks and any juices accumulated on the plate to the pot and nestle the meat pieces in the liquid. Cover the pot and transfer to the oven. Braise for 2 hours. The meat will be very tender, and the sauce will be thick and dark brown.

While the meat is cooking, in a medium saucepan, combine the celery root with cold water to cover. Bring to a boil over high heat,. Reduce the heat to medium-high and simmer until the celery root is tender, about 10 minutes. Drain the celery root in a colander, reserving ¼ cup/60 ml of the cooking water. Return the warm, empty saucepan to the stovetop over an unlit burner. Place the butter in the pan.

Transfer the warm celery root to a blender or food processor and process to a smooth purée. (If using a blender, you will probably need to work in batches.) Add some of the reserved cooking water as needed to reach the desired consistency. Return the purée to the saucepan with the butter. Stir in the cream and ½ tsp salt. Mix well, cover, and set aside until ready to serve.

Gently reheat the celery root purée over medium heat, if necessary. Place a generous portion of the celery root purée on each plate. Place a veal cheek next to the purée. Divide the vegetables from the braising pot between the plates and pour the sauce over the cheeks. Garnish with the parsley and serve at once.

star anise–braised lamb shanks
with butter beans

You'll want to eat this lamb stew with a large spoon in addition to a knife and fork. The spoon will help collect anise-laced juices from the meat and smoky beans. Butter beans and lima beans are similar in texture and taste, but butter beans are lighter in color and larger than the light green beans commonly called limas. Sometimes you'll find so-called butter beans labeled as lima beans anyway. If you can't find true butter beans for this recipe, it's fine to substitute the smaller green bean.

While not complicated, this recipe does require a little forethought. The dried beans are most easily cooked when soaked in water the night prior to use. If you forget to do so, use the shortcut method on page 213. Also, the lamb shanks need to be marinated for at least 6 hours in advance. As the lamb shanks braise in the oven, cook the beans on the stovetop.

These lamb shanks are front-loaded with flavor and eminently suited to a full-bodied red wine accompaniment. Cabernet Sauvignon, Merlot, Cabernet Franc, Syrah, and Petite Sirah would all make an excellent match.

FOR THE LAMB SHANKS:

4 lamb shanks, ¾ to 1 lb/340 to 455 g each

2 yellow onions, coarsely chopped

2 leeks, white parts only, cut into rounds 1 in/2.5 cm thick and rinsed and drained thoroughly

2 carrots, peeled and cut into rounds 1 in/2.5 cm thick

1 head garlic, cut in half horizontally to reveal the interior of each clove

1 bottle (750 ml) dry red wine

Salt and freshly ground pepper

3 star anise pods

1 tsp coriander seeds

3 tbsp extra-virgin olive oil

2 cups/480 ml Chicken Stock (page 216) or canned low-sodium chicken broth

FOR THE BEANS:

2 cups/400 g dried butter beans, soaked overnight in cold water to cover

3 tbsp extra-virgin olive oil

4 bacon/streaky bacon slices, diced

1 yellow onion, chopped

5 garlic cloves, minced

1 carrot, peeled and chopped

3 fresh thyme sprigs, each about 4 in/ 10 cm long

6½ cups/1.4 l Chicken Stock (page 216) or canned low-sodium chicken broth, plus more if needed

Salt

⅓ cup/55 g minced shallots

4 oz/115 g baby shiitake mushrooms, brushed clean and thinly sliced (about 2 cups)

Freshly ground pepper

2 tbsp minced fresh flat-leaf (Italian) parsley

TO MAKE THE LAMB SHANKS: In a large, nonreactive bowl, combine the lamb shanks, onions, leeks, carrots, garlic, and red wine. Cover and let marinate for at least 6 hours or up to 24 hours.

Preheat the oven to 375°F/190°C/gas 5.

Remove the lamb shanks from the marinade and lightly salt and pepper on all sides. Remove the vegetables from the marinade and reserve the liquid and vegetables separately. Wrap the star anise and coriander seeds in cheesecloth/muslin and tie closed to make a bouquet garni. Set aside.

In a Dutch oven or a large, ovenproof saucepan, heat the olive oil over high heat. Add the shanks and sear on all sides until they turn brown and begin to caramelize, about 5 minutes. Transfer to a large plate and set aside.

In the same pot used for searing the shanks, reduce the heat to medium-high and add the vegetables from the marinade. Sauté until the leeks and onions wilt, stirring frequently to prevent burning, about 5 minutes. Add the stock and reserved marinade liquid, raise the heat to high, and bring to a boil. Remove from the heat, add the bouquet garni, and return the lamb shanks to the pot. Cover and transfer to the oven. Braise for 2 hours. Uncover and continue to braise until the meat is very tender and easily falls off the bone, about 30 minutes longer. Remove from the oven, discard the bouquet garni, and cover to keep warm until ready to serve.

TO MAKE THE BEANS: Drain the beans. In a large, heavy-bottomed saucepan or Dutch oven, heat 1 tbsp of the olive oil over medium-high heat. Add the bacon and sauté until crisp, 3 to 4 minutes. Reduce the heat to medium and stir in the onion and garlic. Sauté until the onion is translucent, about 3 minutes. Add the carrot and thyme, stir to mix well, and sauté for 2 minutes. Add 6 cups/ 1.4 l of the stock and bring to a boil over high heat. Add the beans and ½ tsp salt, reduce the heat to low, and cook, uncovered, until the beans are tender, about 1 hour. (If the beans are still not tender after all the liquid is absorbed, add more stock, ½ cup/120 ml at a time, until they are completely tender.) Discard the thyme sprigs.

In a large sauté pan over medium-high heat, heat the remaining 2 tbsp olive oil. Add the shallots and sauté until translucent, about 2 minutes. Stir in the mushrooms, reduce the heat to medium, and cook until wilted, about 2 minutes. Add the remaining ½ cup/120 ml stock and the beans and mix. Reduce the heat to medium-low and simmer until most of the liquid is absorbed, 5 to 10 minutes. Taste and adjust the seasoning with salt and pepper. Cover and set aside until ready to serve.

Reheat the lamb braise and the bean mixture gently over medium heat, if necessary. Place a generous portion of beans on each plate. Place a lamb shank next to the beans. Ladle the lamb braising liquid and vegetables over and around the meat. Garnish with the parsley and serve at once. Pour any extra braising liquid into a small pitcher or gravy boat and pass at the table.

lamb loin

with tabouli, tomatoes, and cannellini beans

With its crunchy cracked wheat, beans, vegetables, and lean lamb loin, this dish is as healthful as it is tasty. Bulgur is made from whole wheat that is steamed, dried, and then cracked. It is the core ingredient for tabouli, which has been a staple in Mediterranean diets for thousands of years. This tabouli can be served at room temperature or just slightly warm. The hot vegetables that sit atop the grains will warm up the tabouli sufficiently on your plate. Purists can cook dried cannellini beans from scratch (see page 213), but with only a small amount required, canned beans will work equally well here, with far less effort and no discernible difference in quality.

The green garlic sauce in this dish was inspired by the fleeting appearance of tender, young, green garlic shoots available only for several weeks each spring. For practical reasons, this version captures the spirit of spring garlic in a sauce that uses ingredients available year-round. This dish is just as good without the garlic sauce, so omit it to save time or to streamline the presentation a bit, if you like.

Any hearty red wine, such as Cabernet Sauvignon or Syrah, will add much to your enjoyment.

FOR THE TABOULI:

½ tsp salt

1 cup/215 g bulgur

¼ cup/60 ml extra-virgin olive oil

2 tbsp fresh lemon juice

2 garlic cloves, minced

⅓ cup/55 g minced red onion

½ English/hothouse cucumber, finely diced (about 1 cup/140 g)

3 tbsp minced fresh chives

¼ cup/7 g minced fresh flat-leaf (Italian) parsley

3 tbsp minced fresh mint

Freshly ground pepper

FOR THE GREEN GARLIC SAUCE (OPTIONAL):

Salt

2 leeks, tender green parts only, cut into slices about 1 in/2.5 cm thick (about 3 cups/340 g) and thoroughly rinsed

1 cup/240 ml firmly packed baby spinach leaves, thoroughly rinsed

1 tbsp unsalted butter

3 garlic cloves, minced

½ cup/120 ml Chicken Stock (page 216) or canned low-sodium chicken broth

½ cup/120 ml heavy (whipping)/double cream

Freshly ground pepper

FOR THE BEANS AND LAMB:

4 tbsp/60 ml extra-virgin olive oil

⅓ cup/55 g diced red onion

2 leeks, white parts only, cut into rounds ¼ in/6 mm thick and rinsed and drained thoroughly

1 cup/200 g cooked cannellini beans (see page 213) or canned cannellini beans, drained and rinsed

½ cup/70 g pitted Kalamata olives, halved

2 cups/340 g cherry tomatoes, halved

3 tbsp minced fresh basil

4 tbsp/55 g unsalted butter

Salt and freshly ground pepper

2 lamb loins, about ½ lb/225 g each

3 garlic cloves, coarsely chopped

4 fresh thyme sprigs

CONTINUED

CHAPTER 8
desserts

A great meal, by definition, is punctuated at the end by something sweet. At *étoile*, we strive to offer our guests a memorable sweet taste that will linger even as they leave the restaurant. That may mean a rich, almost decadent dessert, such as Flourless Chocolate Espresso Cake with Fresh Raspberry Sauce. But just as often, it's something with a lighter touch, such as Bitter Orange Crème Brûlée or the ephemeral Sparkling Wine Granité.

Wine has a place in the sweets department as well. The trick is finding a wine that doesn't overwhelm the dessert, or vice versa. For example, powerful chocolate flavors will most likely cover the nuances found in a late-harvest white wine. As a rule, these elegant, sweet white wines will go best with lighter-styled dishes like Glazed Lemon Pecan Loaf or Orange Chiffon Cake. However, big, bold red dessert wines, such as those made in the style of Port, will stand up well to chocolate and other ultra-rich desserts.

If the evening's showstopper is a rare or highly unusual late-harvest wine—red or white—then it's best to enjoy a simpler dessert that will enhance, but not compete with, what is in the bottle. Lemon Madeleines would be ideal here. These cakelike cookies also go quite well with espresso drinks.

recipes

sparkling wine granité

This refreshing iced treat has a texture similar to a sorbet but is flakier and a bit lighter on the tongue. It can be enjoyed as a palate cleanser between courses, as served at *étoile*, or as a light dessert after a filling meal. Even after adequate time in the freezer, some unfrozen syrup may remain at the bottom of the ice. You can simply spoon it over individual portions for added flavor. At Domaine Chandon, we like to use Chandon Blanc de Noirs as the base wine. But any reasonably dry bubbly will do.

For best results, make the granité a day in advance and just leave it in the freezer overnight.

1 bottle (750 ml) sparkling wine	**1 cup/240 ml sparkling water**
1¾ cups/525 ml Simple Syrup (page 214)	**2 tbsp fresh lemon juice**

In a large bowl or plastic container, combine the sparkling wine, simple syrup, sparkling water, and lemon juice. Stir thoroughly. Cover and place in the freezer until solid, 5 to 6 hours.

To serve, use a spoon or fork to scrape the ice into a martini glass or any other small stemware.

bitter orange crème brûlée

The simple addition of orange zest adds a delightful dimension to this French classic, with tangy citrus notes enhancing the creamy-sweet custard. Home cooks who don't have a chef's blowtorch can easily use their broiler/grill to caramelize the sugar topping. But remember to leave the oven door slightly open and keep watch. A golden sugar crust can quickly turn black if left too long under the flame.

This dessert was born of a collaboration between the cellar and the kitchen. Some years ago during the creation of Chandon Riche—our off dry sparkling wine, which has a hint of sweetness—our winemaker recalled the aromatics issuing from the orange tree that grew not far from the wine cellar. He ran to the kitchen with a bottle of the new wine and asked if the chefs could produce a dessert that evoked the same citrus impression. Bitter Orange Crème Brûlée is now a signature dish at the restaurant.

For a nice pairing with this dessert, add the classic ladyfinger sugar cookies, if you like; they bring a crisp element to join the silky custard and the crunch of the sugar. Make them in advance of the crème brûlée.

FOR THE COOKIES (OPTIONAL):
3 large eggs, separated
½ cup/100 g sugar, plus 2 tbsp
½ tsp vanilla extract/essence
½ cup/60 g all-purpose/plain flour
3 tbsp confectioners'/icing sugar

FOR THE CRÈME BRÛLÉE:
2 cups/480 ml heavy (whipping)/double cream
1 cup/240 ml whole milk
Grated zest from two oranges
12 large egg yolks
½ cup/100 g sugar, plus 6 tbsp/75 g
Sprigs of fresh mint or chocolate mint, for garnish

TO MAKE THE COOKIES (IF USING): Preheat the oven to 350°F/180°C/gas 4. Line a baking sheet/tray with parchment/baking paper.

In a large bowl, using an electric mixer, beat the egg yolks with the ½ cup/100 g sugar until the mixture turns pale yellow, about 1 minute. Add the vanilla and beat until the batter gets very thick, about 1 to 2 minutes longer. Using a rubber spatula, add the flour and mix slowly and gently into the yolk mixture, just until it's barely incorporated. (It is important not to overmix; some of the flour should still be visible along the edges and in the center of the bowl.)

In a clean bowl, using the electric mixer and clean beaters, beat the egg whites with the 2 tbsp sugar until soft peaks form. Using the rubber spatula, gently fold the egg-white mixture into the batter. Do not stir vigorously.

Using a ladle, in small batches if necessary, carefully scoop the batter into a pastry/piping bag with a size 4 tip. Pipe thin lines of batter about 3 in/7.5 cm long and ¼ in/6 mm thick onto the prepared baking sheet/tray, spacing them about 1 in/25 mm apart. Use a sifter or fine-mesh sieve to dust the cookies with the confectioners'/icing sugar.

CONTINUED

Bake until golden, 10 to 12 minutes. Remove the tray from the oven and let the cookies cool on the pan for about 1 minute to allow them to firm up a bit. Using a spatula, carefully transfer to a wire rack to cool completely. Repeat to use the remaining batter. You should have 25 to 30 cookies.

TO MAKE THE CRÈME BRÛLÉE: Preheat the oven to 300°F/150°C/gas 2.

In a medium saucepan, combine the cream, milk, and orange zest and heat until steam begins to rise. Do not let boil. Remove from the heat and nestle the pot in an ice bath. Let stand, stirring occasionally, until the cream mixture cools to room temperature, 5 to 10 minutes.

While the cream mixture is cooling, in a large bowl, combine the egg yolks and the ½ cup/ 100 g sugar. Whisk until the sugar is dissolved and thoroughly blended with the yolks. Gently whisk in the cream mixture.

Pour the custard through a fine-mesh sieve set over a large glass measuring pitcher or bowl with a pouring lip to strain out any solids. Divide the custard evenly among six 4-oz/120-ml rame-kins. Place in a roasting pan/tray and add water to come 1 in/2.5 cm up the sides of the ramekins. Bake until the custards are firm, 35 to 40 minutes. Remove from the oven and let cool in the water bath to room temperature. Cover with plastic wrap/cling film and refrigerate until well chilled, at least 2 hours and up to 2 days.

To serve, remove the plastic wrap/cling film and gently lay a paper towel/absorbent paper on top of each custard. Gently press down on the towel to remove any moisture buildup, being care-ful not to dent the custard. Sprinkle 1 tbsp sugar evenly over each custard. Using a blowtorch, pass the flame above the sugar until it melts and turns golden brown. (Alternatively, preheat the broiler/ grill and slip the custards under the broiler 4 to 6 in/10 to 15 cm from the heat source to melt the sugar; leave the oven door open slightly and watch closely, as the sugar can scorch suddenly.) Let the crème brûlée stand at room temperature until the sugar hardens, 1 to 2 minutes.

If serving with the sugar cookies, lay 2 cookies over each custard, leaning them on the edge of the ramekins and garnish with the mint. Serve at once. Enjoy any extra cookies the following day or with a sweet, dessert wine.

white chocolate mousse
with rum

This velvety-smooth dessert is surprisingly light on the tongue. Whipped cream makes the mousse particularly airy, while the rum creates a sweet earthiness. It's easy to prepare and even easier to eat.

4 oz/113 g white chocolate, coarsely chopped

2 large eggs, plus 2 large egg yolks

1 cup/240 ml heavy (whipping)/
double cream

1 envelope (2½ tsp) unflavored gelatin

3 tbsp light rum

18 to 24 fresh raspberries

Fill the bottom of a double boiler with enough water to reach the bottom of the top pan and insert the top pan. (Alternatively, fill a saucepan with enough water to reach the bottom of a smaller saucepan nested inside or a stainless-steel bowl fit snugly over the top and insert the small saucepan or bowl.) Bring the water to a simmer over medium-high heat, then reduce the heat to medium-low. Do not let the water boil vigorously.

Put the white chocolate in the top bowl of the double boiler and heat, stirring frequently with a rubber spatula, until the chocolate is thoroughly melted and smooth. When the chocolate has melted, reduce the heat to medium-low to keep it warm.

Place the top pan of a second double boiler on a work surface. In the bottom of the double boiler, bring about 1 in/2.5 cm water to a simmer over medium-high heat, then reduce the heat to medium. In the top half of the double boiler, combine the eggs and egg yolks. Whisk to blend, then place over the simmering water. (Alternatively, bring about 1 in/2.5 cm of water to a simmer in a saucepan. Combine the eggs and egg yolks in a stainless-steel bowl and nest the bowl snugly over the top of the saucepan.) Cook, whisking occasionally, until warm to the touch, 3 to 5 minutes.

While the eggs and chocolate are on the stovetop, in a medium bowl, using an electric mixer, beat the cream until stiff peaks form.

Transfer the warmed eggs to a large bowl and use a whisk or the electric mixer with clean beaters to beat the eggs until frothy. Add the gelatin and melted chocolate to the eggs. Beat the mixture until thoroughly blended. Mix in the rum. Using a rubber spatula, gently fold in the whipped cream.

Divide the mousse into 6 shallow dessert bowls or wineglasses. Use a paper towel/absorbent paper to wipe any mousse that spills on the sides of the bowls or glasses. Cover each bowl or glass with plastic wrap/cling film and refrigerate for at least 3 hours or up to overnight. When ready to serve, garnish each dessert with 3 or 4 fresh raspberries. Serve chilled.

risotto pudding
with sun-dried cherries and mascarpone whipped cream

This is not your average savory risotto. Mildly sweet and infused with dried cherries, the rice grains are cooked al dente to maintain a firm, crunchy character. They are then smothered in a lush mascarpone whipped cream—a richer, thicker version of traditional whipped cream—that presides over the top and slowly melts into the risotto as you eat.

In order for the mascarpone to melt, the risotto must be served warm. To this end, serve the pudding shortly after it is made, or refrigerate for up to 24 hours and reheat in a microwave.

5 cups/1.2 l whole milk	1 cup/215 g Arborio rice
¼ cup/50 g sugar, plus 2 tsp	½ cup/85 g chopped dried cherries
½ vanilla bean/pod, scraped (see page 214), or 1 tsp vanilla extract/essence	¼ cup/110 g mascarpone cheese
2 tbsp unsalted butter	½ cup/120 ml heavy (whipping)/ double cream

In a medium saucepan over medium heat, whisk together the milk and the ¼ cup/50 g sugar. Add the vanilla and heat until steam begins to rise. Do not let boil. (Discard the vanilla bean, if using.) Reduce the heat to low and cover to keep warm.

In a large saucepan, melt the butter over medium-high heat. Add the rice and stir to coat the grains with the melted butter. Add ½ cup/120 ml of the warm milk mixture and stir frequently—but not constantly—until the liquid is absorbed, about 3 minutes. If necessary, reduce the heat so that the milk simmers but does not boil. Continue adding the warm milk mixture, ½ cup at a time and stirring frequently until most of the liquid is absorbed before adding more, until you have used 3 cups/720 ml.

Stir in the dried cherries. Continue to add the remaining 2 cups/480 ml milk in ½-cup/ 120-ml increments, stirring frequently as before. The rice is done when it is tender but still slightly firm at the center of each grain. Remove from the heat, cover, and set aside.

In a bowl, combine the mascarpone cheese, cream, and the 2 tsp sugar. Using an electric mixer, beat until stiff peaks form.

Divide the warm rice pudding among individual bowls and top each portion with a large dollop of mascarpone whipped cream. Serve at once.

frozen cappuccino soufflés

in chocolate cups

If you like cappuccino, you'll surely love this frozen version, a picturesque and impressive frozen chocolate cup made of rich bittersweet chocolate and filled with frosty and frothy espresso soufflé. It's a sweet dessert, but still light on the palate.

Using a double boiler helps prevent the chocolate from burning; if you don't have one, you can rig a simple double boiler with other tools in your kitchen: just place the chocolate in a small saucepan and nest it in a larger saucepan partially filled with boiling water. To warm the egg yolks, you can simulate a double boiler by using a stainless-steel bowl and a saucepan in which the bowl fits snugly on top.

9 oz/255 g bittersweet chocolate, cut into 1-in/2.5-cm chunks

1½ cups/360 ml heavy (whipping)/ double cream

3 tbsp instant espresso powder

4 large eggs, separated, plus 1 whole large egg

¾ cup/150 g sugar, plus 2 tbsp

1 envelope (2½ tsp) unflavored gelatin

2 oz/55 g semisweet/plain chocolate, grated

Have ready 8 small (5-oz/150-ml) wax-coated paper drinking cups.

Fill the bottom of a double boiler with enough water to reach the bottom of the top pan and insert the top pan. Bring the water to a simmer over medium-high heat and then reduce the heat to medium-low. Do not let the water boil vigorously.

Put the bittersweet chocolate in the top bowl of the double boiler and heat, stirring frequently with a rubber spatula, until the chocolate is thoroughly melted and smooth. Maintain a gentle simmer to prevent the chocolate from hardening.

Place one of the paper cups on its side on a clean work surface. Using a soupspoon or table-spoon, carefully spoon about 1 tbsp of the melted chocolate into the cup and carefully roll and tip the cup to coat the sides, but leaving a ½-in/12-mm rim uncoated at the mouth of the cup. Add another 1 tbsp melted chocolate and again gently roll the cup to cover the sides with a second coat and to coat the bottom this time, still leaving the rim around the top uncoated. Place the coated cup, still on its side, on a plate. Repeat to coat the remaining cups. When the chocolate has hardened enough to stop running, place the coated paper cups upright in the freezer until ready to use.

In a medium bowl, combine 1 cup/240 ml of the cream and the espresso powder. Using an electric mixer, beat until soft peaks form, 1 to 2 minutes. Set aside.

CONTINUED

Place the top pan of a clean double boiler on a work surface. In the bottom of the double boiler, bring about 1 in/2.5 cm water to a simmer over medium-high heat, then reduce the heat to medium. In the top half of the double boiler, combine the 4 egg yolks, the whole egg, and the ¾ cup/150 g sugar. Whisk to blend, then place over the simmering water. Cook, whisking gently and constantly, for 10 minutes. The mixture will become frothy. Remove from the heat and set aside.

In a small bowl, using a fork, stir together the gelatin with 2 to 3 tablespoons hot water. It should become thick and sticky. Scrape the gelatin into the egg-yolk mixture and whisk vigorously to mix well.

In a clean large bowl, using the electric mixer and clean beaters, beat the egg whites with the 2 tbsp sugar until stiff peaks form, about 1 minute. Using a rubber spatula, fold the egg-gelatin mixture into the egg whites. Fold in the espresso whipped cream. Remove the chocolate-coated paper cups from the freezer. Using a ladle or measuring cup, pour the soufflé base into the cups, filling each to the rim. Return the filled cups to the freezer and freeze until the soufflés are firm to the touch, 3 to 4 hours. (You can freeze the soufflés for up to 48 hours, but they will lose their lightness, with the consistency changing to something more akin to ice cream.)

Using an electric mixer, beat the remaining ½ cup/120 ml cream until soft peaks form, about 2 minutes. Set aside. Remove the frozen cappuccino cups from the freezer. Carefully insert the tip of a paring knife into the side of each paper cup, just above the bottom. Gently pry open and tear off the bottom of the cups and then peel away the sides of each cup to reveal the frozen, molded chocolate. Place a cappuccino cup on each of 8 small dessert plates. Top each with a small dollop of the whipped cream and sprinkle with the grated chocolate. Serve at once.

bittersweet chocolate soufflé

This dark chocolate dessert somehow maintains the lightness of a soufflé without losing its satisfying richness. As you eat, you'll discover the flavored nuances of great chocolate—a good reason to use a top-notch brand of cocoa powder.

After blending the chocolate with the egg whites, don't worry if the mix seems too lumpy. It will smooth out as it bakes. Also, remember that some liquid chocolate may remain inside the soufflés when they are ready to serve. Finally, don't be afraid to let the soufflés cool for at least 5 minutes before serving. Their cups may fall slightly, but they do need to solidify—and hopefully, this cooling-off period will also prevent overenthusiastic chocolate aficionados from burning their tongues.

2 cups/480 ml whole milk

1 vanilla bean/pod split and scraped (see page 214) or 1 tsp vanilla extract/essence

¾ cup/150 g granulated sugar

6 large eggs, separated, plus 4 large egg whites

¼ cup/30 g all-purpose/plain flour

1½ cups/150 g unsweetened cocoa powder, preferably Dutch process

1 tbsp butter, at room temperature

¼ cup/20 g confectioners'/icing sugar

In a medium saucepan over medium heat, combine the milk, vanilla, and ¼ cup/50 g of the granulated sugar and bring to a gentle boil, stirring occasionally. Remove from the heat and let cool to room temperature. (If using the vanilla bean, remove it from the milk mixture and discard.)

In a medium bowl, whisk the egg yolks with ¼ cup/50 g of the granulated sugar until they are pale yellow and a ribbon is formed when the whisk is lifted above the bowl. Sift the flour (or if you don't have a sifter, just make sure the flour is clump-free) and whisk it into the egg yolk mixture. Continue to whisk while slowly adding about half of the milk mixture. Set aside.

Return the saucepan with the remaining milk mixture to the stovetop and bring to a boil over medium-high heat. Reduce the heat to low and slowly add the egg yolk mixture, whisking continuously for 4 to 5 minutes, until thickened to a pudding-like consistency. Remove from the heat and whisk in the cocoa powder. The "pudding" will become very thick. Set aside.

Preheat the oven to 375°F/190°C/gas 5. Grease six 4-oz/120-ml ramekins with the butter and set aside.

In a large bowl, using an electric mixer, beat the egg whites until foamy. Add the remaining ¼ cup/50 g granulated sugar and continue to beat the egg whites until they form stiff peaks. Whisk the cocoa pudding into the egg whites and mix well.

Fill each ramekin to the top with the soufflé mix and smooth flat with a rubber spatula. Place the ramekins on a baking sheet/tray on the bottom rack in the oven. Bake until the soufflés have risen ¼ to ½ in/6 to 12 mm above each ramekin and the tops no longer jiggle in a liquidy manner, 15 to 20 minutes. (They will still be soft to the touch, however.) Remove from the oven and let cool for at least 5 minutes to firm up.

Dust the top of each soufflé with the confectioners'/icing sugar. Serve warm or let cool to room temperature.

lemon madeleines

French author Marcel Proust famously set the stage for his celebrated novel *Remembrance of Things Past* in an epiphany-induced encounter with "plump little cakes which look as though they had been molded in the fluted valve of a scallop shell." We can't guarantee the same revelatory experience with these buttery biscuits. But there is a reason "petites Madeleines" are so well loved in France—and at *étoile*. They are simply delicious, especially when imbued with a subtle hint of lemon.

Proust enjoyed his madeleine with a cup of tea, indeed an excellent accompaniment. But a late-harvest, honeyed dessert wine would also provide a foil for great pleasure and possibly further existential discourse. To make these little cakes, you'll need to purchase a madeleine baking mold, commonly found in shops that sell kitchenware and baking utensils.

2 tbsp unsalted butter, at room temperature, plus ½ cup/115 g

1½ cups/195 g all-purpose/plain flour

½ tsp baking powder

Pinch of salt

⅔ cup/130 g sugar

3 large eggs

1 tsp vanilla extract/essence

2 tsp grated lemon zest

Preheat the oven to 325°F/165°C/gas 3.

Grease the madeleine mold with the 2 tbsp butter and dust with ½ cup/65 g of the flour. Turn the mold upside down and tap to remove excess flour. In a medium bowl, sift together the remaining 1 cup/130 g flour, the baking powder, and the salt. Set aside.

In a large bowl, using an electric mixer, beat the ½ cup/115 g butter with the sugar until pale yellow in color. Add the eggs, vanilla, and lemon zest and beat until creamy white.

Pour the flour mixture into the butter mixture. Use a whisk to mix the batter thoroughly. Place 1 tbsp batter in the center of each madeleine mold. Bake until the edges of the cakes start to turn golden brown, leaving the centers moist and spongy, 12 to 14 minutes.

Transfer to a wire rack/cake cooler and let cool for about 2 minutes, then use a fork to gently pry the little cakes from their molds.

passion fruit cheesecake

Passion fruit is blessed with zippy acidity and sensuous herbal and citrus flavors, which give this cheese-cake a unique character. You'll find passion fruit juice concentrate in most specialty-food shops. The sour-cream topping adds a welcome lightness that's lacking in more conventional cheesecakes. At the restaurant, we make it in individual molds (as pictured), but for the home kitchen we have given it a more conventional pie form.

FOR THE CRUST:

15 graham crackers/digestive biscuits, broken into pieces

¼ cup/50 g granulated sugar

½ cup/115 g unsalted butter, melted

FOR THE FILLING:

1 lb/455 g cream cheese, at room temperature

1 cup/100 g confectioners'/icing sugar

1½ tsp vanilla extract/essence

3 large eggs

½ cup/120 ml passion-fruit juice concentrate, diluted with ½ cup/120 ml water

¼ cup/55 g sour cream, plus 2½ cups/570 g

⅓ cup/85 g mascarpone cheese

¼ cup/60 ml heavy (whipping)/double cream

1 cup/200 g granulated sugar

TO MAKE THE CRUST: Preheat the oven to 325°F/165°C/gas 3.

In a blender or food processor, process the graham cracker/digestive biscuit pieces into coarse crumbs. In a large bowl, combine the crumbs with the sugar and stir with a wooden spoon to mix thoroughly. Pour in the melted butter and continue to stir until well blended. The mixture should stick together when squeezed firmly in your hand.

Transfer the graham-cracker mixture to a 9-in/23-cm springform pan/tin, distributing it evenly on the surface. Pat and press the crumb mixture firmly onto the bottom and about 1 in/2.5 cm up the sides of the tin. Bake until golden brown, about 8 minutes. Remove from the oven and let cool slightly. When cool enough to handle, wrap the bottom and sides of the tin with a large piece of heavy-duty aluminum foil, crimping the sides so the foil fits snugly. (This will prevent water from running into the bottom seam while baking in the water bath.) Set aside.

Preheat the oven to 300°F/150°C/gas 2.

CONTINUED

TO MAKE THE FILLING: In a large bowl, using an electric mixer, beat together the cream cheese, confectioners'/icing sugar, and 1 tsp of the vanilla until thick and creamy, about 1 minute. Use a rubber spatula to scrape down the sides of the bowl as needed. Add the eggs, one at a time, and continue mixing until they are well incorporated. The mixture should be pale yellow in color.

Add the diluted passion fruit juice and continue beating, scraping down the sides of the bowl as needed. Add the ¼ cup/55 g sour cream and the mascarpone cheese and beat until blended. Add the cream and beat for 1 minute longer. Place the springform pan/tin with the graham cracker crust in a larger baking dish. Pour the cream cheese mixture into the crust. Add warm water to the baking dish so that it comes halfway up the sides of the springform pan/tin.

Carefully set the baking dish on the middle rack of the oven and bake until the cream cheese mixture is fairly firm, about 1 hour. (It might still jiggle a bit.) Keep the cake tin in the water bath and remove from the oven; leave the oven on. Let cool for 20 to 30 minutes.

In a medium bowl, using the electric mixer and clean beaters, beat together the remaining 2½ cups/570 g sour cream with the granulated sugar and the remaining ½ tsp vanilla. Continue to beat until creamy textured. Pour the sour cream mixture on top of the cooled cake and return the cake pan in the water bath to the oven. Bake until the top is firm but still somewhat soft to the touch, about 25 minutes. Turn off the oven and leave the door slightly open. Let the cake cool in the oven for 30 minutes.

Remove the cake from the water bath and place on a countertop on top of a kitchen towel. Remove the aluminum foil, which might allow some water to escape. Transfer the cake (still in the springform) to the refrigerator and chill for at least 8 hours or up to 2 days.

To serve, run the edge of a warm knife along the inside edges of the pan/tin. Remove the sides and cut the cake into wedges.

glazed lemon pecan loaf

Light and lemony with crunchy pecans, this is a dessert that goes well with sweet wine. Try a sweet sparkler or a late-harvest white to finish your meal in style. Or just enjoy a piece of cake for a mid-afternoon snack with your beverage of choice.

Cooking spray or canola oil for greasing

1½ cups/195 g all-purpose/plain flour

1 tbsp baking powder

⅛ tsp salt

½ cup/115 g unsalted butter, at room temperature

1 cup/200 g granulated sugar

2 large eggs

½ cup/120 ml whole milk

½ cup/55 g finely chopped pecans

½ cup/120 ml fresh lemon juice

1 tbsp grated lemon zest

¼ cup/20 g confectioners'/icing sugar, plus 2 tbsp

Preheat the oven to 325°F/165°C/gas 3. Lightly grease a 9-by-5-in/23-by-12-cm loaf pan/tin with cooking spray.

In a medium bowl, whisk together the flour, baking powder, and salt. Set aside.

In a large bowl, using an electric mixer, beat the butter and granulated sugar together until pale yellow in color. Add the eggs and beat until well combined, 1 to 2 minutes. Add the dry ingredients and beat to combine thoroughly, about 2 minutes longer. Add the milk and beat to combine, using a rubber spatula as needed to scrape down the sides of the bowl. Add the pecans and mix well. Add ¼ cup/60 ml of the lemon juice and the lemon zest. Continue to beat until smooth, about 1 minute longer.

Scrape the batter into the prepared pan and smooth the top with the rubber spatula. Bake until firm and a toothpick inserted into the center comes out clean, 55 to 60 minutes. The top should be lightly golden and springy to the touch in the middle. Transfer to a wire rack/cake cooler and let cool for 5 minutes.

Turn the cake out from the pan/tin onto a large plate, then carefully turn the cake right-side up. In a small glass bowl, combine the remaining ¼ cup/60 ml lemon juice and the ¼ cup/20 g confectioners'/icing sugar. Whisk until the sugar is not lumpy. Using a pastry brush, brush the lemon glaze on the top and sides of the loaf.

Let the cake stand at room temperature to absorb the glaze, 2 to 3 hours. Dust with the 2 tbsp confectioners'/icing sugar, cut into slices, and serve.

orange chiffon cake

Bursting with orange flavors and topped with a Grand Marnier whipped cream, this light, classic chiffon cake is perfect on its own. But it would also pair well with any number of late-harvest dessert wines — particularly those made from orange-scented Muscat grapes.

Cakes baked in a chiffon, or tube, cake pan/tin are not supposed to stick when they are turned over for removal. But just to make sure yours doesn't stick, we recommend using a neutral spray oil, such as grapeseed, which can be purchased at most grocery stores. It will evenly and easily coat the surface of the vessel with a minimal amount of oil. If you can't find a spray oil, lightly grease with butter.

Cooking spray oil or butter for greasing

2½ cups/285 g cake/soft-wheat flour

1½ cups/300 g granulated sugar

1 tbsp baking powder

1 tsp salt

5 large egg yolks

½ cup/120 ml canola oil

½ cup/55 g chopped orange zest (from about 3 oranges)

¾ cup/180 ml fresh orange juice

8 large egg whites

½ tsp cream of tartar

3 tbsp confectioners'/icing sugar

1 cup/240 ml heavy (whipping)/ double cream

1 tbsp Grand Marnier liqueur

Preheat the oven to 325°F/165°C/gas 3. Lightly grease a 10-in/25-cm chiffon or tube cake pan/ tin with cooking spray oil. In a large bowl, whisk together the flour, granulated sugar, baking powder, and salt. In a medium bowl, using an electric mixer, beat the egg yolks, canola oil, orange zest, and orange juice until frothy and pale orange in color, about 1 minute.

In another medium bowl, using the electric mixer, and clean beaters, beat the egg whites with the cream of tartar until soft peaks form, about 1 minute. Set aside. Using the electric mixer, gradually mix the egg-yolk mixture into the flour mixture. Beat until the ingredients are thoroughly blended and a smooth batter forms, about 2 minutes. Using a rubber spatula, fold the egg whites gently into the batter just until no streaks remain.

Scrape the batter into the prepared pan/tin and place on the middle rack of the oven. Bake until golden brown and the center is firm yet spongy to the touch, about 1 hour. Remove the cake from the oven and immediately invert onto an oiled wire rack/cake cooler. As the cake cools and firms up, it will drop out of the cake pan/tin. Remove the cake pan/tin and turn the cake right-side up onto a large serving plate. When the cake has cooled completely, dust with the confectioners'/icing sugar.

In a medium bowl, combine the cream and Grand Marnier. Using an electric mixer, beat until soft peaks form, 2 to 3 minutes.

To serve, cut the cake into slices and top with a dollop of whipped cream.

polenta cake

Buttery, moist, sweet—and with just a little crunch—this rustic cake is topped with luscious brandied black-berries, which we make using our own Domaine Chandon Brandy. Sip a sweet white still or sparkling wine or a red dessert wine as an accompaniment. And, yes, we really mean it: the recipe calls for 5 cups confectioners' sugar.

Cooking spray oil or canola oil for greasing

2 cups/255 g bread/strong flour

1 cup/140 g polenta

1½ cups/340 g unsalted butter, at room temperature

5 cups/500 g confectioners'/icing sugar

⅛ tsp vanilla seeds, scraped from a vanilla bean/pod (see page 214)

4 large eggs, plus 2 egg yolks

4 cups/455 g blackberries

½ cup/100 g granulated sugar

2 tbsp brandy

Preheat the oven to 325°F/165°C/gas 3. Lightly grease a 9-in/23-cm springform cake pan/tin with cooking spray oil.

Sift the flour into a medium bowl. Add the polenta and stir to mix well. Set aside.

In a large bowl, using an electric mixer, beat the butter, confectioners'/icing sugar, and vanilla together until pale yellow and creamy, about 2 minutes. Use a rubber spatula to scrape down the sides of the bowl as needed. Add the eggs and egg yolks and continue to beat for 2 minutes longer. Using the rubber spatula, fold the dry ingredients into the butter mixture. The batter will be fairly thick, but stir to mix thoroughly.

Scrape the batter into the prepared pan/tin. Smooth the top of the cake with the rubber spatula. Bake until the cake is firm and a toothpick inserted into the center comes out clean, about 1 hour. Transfer to a wire rack/cake cooler and let cool slightly. When cool enough to touch, unmold the cake onto a serving plate. Let cool completely before cutting.

While the cake is cooling, in a medium saucepan over medium-low heat, combine the black-berries, granulated sugar, and brandy. Using a hand-held potato masher or a large fork, mash the berries to break them up. Cook, stirring constantly, until the sugar is completely dissolved and most of the blackberries have broken down into a juicy sauce, about 5 minutes. Remove from the heat and let cool to lukewarm before serving.

To serve, cut the cake into wedges and drizzle with the blackberry sauce.

hazelnut cake
with cocoa butter icing

This light-bodied layer cake is not too sweet, a fact that allows us to better appreciate the subtle flavors in the creamy cocoa butter icing. Nonetheless, it won't disappoint those with a sweet tooth. Let's just say the cake's diverse flavor profile—and not its sweetness—is exceptional. A few tips will help you in the kitchen: Patience is the key. Don't be in a rush to open the oven door when monitoring the baking. Wait at least 20 minutes or the cake halves may collapse in the oven. And remember to wait for the freshly baked cake to fully cool down before applying the icing, or your icing will melt.

FOR THE CAKE:

2 tbsp unsalted butter, at room temperature

2 tbsp cake/soft-wheat flour, plus 2 cups/225 g, sifted

10 large eggs, separated

1½ cups/300 g granulated sugar

2 tsp vanilla extract/essence

½ cup/120 ml boiling water

1 cup/115 g finely ground hazelnuts

2 tsp baking powder

Salt

FOR THE ICING:

1 cup/225 g unsalted butter, at room temperature

1 large egg yolk

2 cups/200 g confectioners'/icing sugar

3 tbsp unsweetened cocoa powder

½ tsp vanilla extract/essence

½ cup/120 ml heavy (whipping)/ double cream

¼ cup/30 g coarsely ground hazelnuts

TO MAKE THE CAKE: Preheat the oven to 350°F/180°C/gas 4.

Grease the bottoms and sides of two 9-in/23-cm cake pans/tins with the 2 tbsp butter and sprinkle the pan surfaces with the 2 tbsp flour. Turn the pans upside down and gently tap them to remove excess flour. Set aside.

In a large bowl, combine the egg yolks, 1 cup/200 g of the granulated sugar, and the vanilla. Using an electric mixer, beat until pale yellow in color, about 1 minute. Continue mixing while slowly adding ¼ cup/60 ml of the boiling water, making sure that the egg yolks do not cook. Repeat this step with the remaining ¼ cup boiling water. Beat until thoroughly incorporated, about 2 minutes. Add the 2 cups/225 g flour, the hazelnuts, the baking powder, and a pinch of salt. Beat to mix well, about 2 minutes longer.

In another large mixing bowl, using the electric mixer with clean beaters, beat the egg whites and the remaining ½ cup/100 g granulated sugar until stiff peaks form, about 1 minute. Use a rubber spatula to fold small batches of the egg white mixture into the cake batter until the egg whites are fully incorporated.

Divide the batter evenly between the two prepared cake pans/tins. Place on the middle rack of the oven and bake until the tops are golden brown, the middle is firm, and a toothpick inserted into the center comes out clean, 25 to 30 minutes. (Do not open the oven door during the first 20 minutes baking time; the cake batter could fall.) Remove the cakes from the oven and let cool for 15 minutes. Invert each cake over a plate to remove from the pans/tins. Let cool completely, about 40 minutes, before turning them back upright.

If the tops of the cakes are still rounded and not flat, use a long, sharp knife to slice off a thin layer from the top of one cake, thus flattening it and making it easier for stacking later. The flattened cake will become the bottom half when the cake is assembled.

TO MAKE THE ICING: In a large bowl, using an electric mixer, beat the butter, egg yolk, confectioners'/ icing sugar, and cocoa powder. Beat until well mixed, about 1 minute. Add the vanilla and cream and continue to mix until the icing is smooth and creamy, about 2 minutes longer.

To frost the cake, first apply the icing to the cake to be used for the bottom half of the assembled cake. Use a flat rubber spatula to lay a thick (about ½ in/12 mm) layer of icing over the cake top. Coat the sides with a thinner layer (about ⅛ to ¼ in/3 to 6 mm) thick. Carefully place the second, unfrosted cake on top of the frosted one, setting the flat bottom against the flat, frosted top. Cover the top and sides of the second layer with the icing. Smooth out to evenly coat the entire cake. Sprinkle the cake top with the ground hazelnuts.

Keep refrigerated until ready to eat, or up to 24 hours. Bring to room temperature, about 30 minutes, before serving.

flourless chocolate espresso cake

with fresh raspberry sauce

This creamy, mocha-flavored cake gets a fruity lift from the intense raspberry sauce that accompanies it. It's the perfect partnership of two very diverse tastes. Homemade whipped cream tops it off, creating a wholly satisfying mealtime finale.

10 oz/280 g bittersweet chocolate, cut into large chunks

¼ cup/60 ml Kahlúa liqueur

¼ cup/60 ml brewed espresso coffee

6 large eggs

¾ cup/150 g sugar, plus 2 tbsp

1 cup/240 ml heavy (whipping)/double cream

1 tbsp unsalted butter

4 cups/455 g fresh raspberries

Preheat the oven to 375°F/190°C/gas 5.

In a nonstick saucepan, melt the chocolate with the Kahlúa and espresso over low heat, stirring gently to break up clumps of chocolate and maintain a smooth consistency. While the chocolate is melting, in a large bowl, whisk together the eggs and ½ cup/100 g of the sugar until pale yellow in color. When the chocolate is completely melted, remove from the heat and let cool slightly, about 2 minutes. Pour the melted chocolate into the egg mixture, stirring with a whisk to mix.

In a medium bowl, beat ½ cup/120 ml of the cream with an electric mixer or handheld whisk until the cream becomes stiff and peaks form. Use a rubber spatula to gently fold the whipped cream into the chocolate-and-egg mixture until the cream is thoroughly blended into the chocolate.

Use the butter to grease the bottom and sides of a 9-in/23-cm springform pan/tin. Pour the batter into the pan/tin and bake until a toothpick inserted into the center comes out dry, about 25 minutes. Let cool for 15 minutes before removing the cake from the springform. If not serving immediately, cover and refrigerate for up to 24 hours. Remove from the refrigerator 15 minutes prior to serving.

While the cake is baking, in a medium nonstick saucepan over medium heat, combine the raspberries and ¼ cup/50 g of the sugar. Stir frequently as the raspberries break down to become a sauce, about 5 minutes. As soon as small bubbles appear, reduce the heat to maintain a gentle simmer and continue to simmer for 10 minutes, stirring occasionally. Remove from the heat and transfer to a blender. Pulse 6 to 8 times until the sauce becomes fairly smooth. (Keep the blender top covered to prevent any hot sauce from splashing out.) Pour the sauce into a container, cover, and let cool. Refrigerate until ready to use, or up to 24 hours.

To serve, using an electric mixer or handheld whisk, beat the remaining ½ cup/120 ml cream with the remaining 2 tbsp sugar until the cream becomes stiff and peaks form. Cut the cake into eight wedge-shaped slices. Place a piece of cake on each plate, topped with a large dollop of fresh whipped cream. Drizzle the raspberry sauce onto each plate.

pear clafouti

The word *clafouti* is derived from a Provençal word that means "to fill." Yet this lovely, light custard-based pear tart is hardly filling. Perhaps that's why it makes such a perfect ending to a fine meal. A hint of anise pairs beautifully with the pears, all nicely framed in the baked custard.

Because clafouti is not terribly sweet, it will not overwhelm a fine white dessert wine, such as a late-harvest Muscat, Riesling, or Gewürztraminer.

1 tbsp unsalted butter, at room temperature

1 tbsp granulated sugar, plus 1 cup/200 g

3 large eggs

Seeds of 1 vanilla bean/pod (see page 214) or ½ tsp vanilla extract/essence

½ cup/65 g all-purpose/plain flour

1 cup/240 ml heavy (whipping)/double cream

1½ tsp fennel seeds

1 tbsp brandy

3 Bartlett/Williams' pears

1 tbsp confectioners'/icing sugar

Preheat the oven to 400°F/200°C/gas 6.

Grease a 10-in/25-cm round or square baking dish with the butter and sprinkle it with the 1 tbsp granulated sugar. Turn the baking dish upside down and gently tap to remove excess sugar.

In a large bowl, using an electric mixer, beat the eggs until frothy. With the mixer running, add the vanilla, the 1 cup/200 g granulated sugar, and the flour. Continue to beat until the flour is well incorporated and the mixture is pale yellow, about 45 seconds. Add the cream, fennel seeds, and brandy. Beat until well blended, about 1 minute. Set aside and let stand at room temperature for 15 minutes.

While the batter is resting, peel, core, and cut the pears into thin, lengthwise slices. Place the sliced pears, slightly overlapping each other, on the bottom of the baking dish to create a spiral pattern or other design of your choice. Pour the batter over the pears and bake until golden brown on top and fairly firm to the touch, about 45 minutes.

Transfer to a wire rack/cake cooler and let cool to room temperature, about 1 hour. It will continue to firm up slightly. Dust with a light sprinkling of confectioners'/icing sugar. To serve, cut into individual portions or scoop out from the baking dish with a large spoon.

basics: tips and techniques

A good home cook keeps a small collection of basic techniques in his or her repertoire and essential supplies at the ready. Typically, they provide simple solutions to aid in the creation of a more complex dish.

Perhaps the easiest—and most important—recipes in this chapter are the stocks. They require little more than scraps or leftovers to prepare. Yet they provide an important foundation for many of the soups and sauces found in the book. Stocks also freeze well for up to 3 months, so you can store them in batches. They will serve you well not only for various recipes here, but also in general. If you substitute store-bought broth or stock, make sure you use one that is low in salt and clearly marked "low sodium" or the equivalent. A high-sodium commercial broth may throw off the salt measurements in a recipe.

Making great meals at home does not require a team of chefs, a 6-burner stove, or an extensive collection of pots and pans. But a limited number of key items will definitely help you in the kitchen. A 3-qt/3-l saucepan and a 4- to 6-qt/4- to 6-l pot will come in very handy. So will a small sauté pan (8 to 12 in/ 20 to 30 cm in diameter) and a large frying pan (at least 16 in/40 cm in diameter). A few baking dishes and cake pans/tins, some sharp knives, a stainless-steel colander, a small strainer, a slotted spoon and a few wooden spoons, cooking tongs, a rubber and a metal spatula, and a blender will allow you to make nearly every dish in this book. For braising in the oven or on the stovetop, a Dutch oven can also be very useful.

Finally, remember that the ingredients in recipes are listed in the order they are needed. For greatest ease in the kitchen, prepare your ingredients in advance and lay them out as you will require them.

Cooking at home should be fun. The suggestions made here or found on page 58 will help make gatherings at your house most enjoyable for everyone.

recipes

toasting nuts and seeds

Toasting nuts or seeds highlights their aromas and also adds additional crunchiness to their texture. This simple technique requires nothing more than a sauté pan or small frying pan—but remain vigilant and *do not* let your nuts or seeds burn. It can happen quite suddenly after you have achieved the perfect toastiness.

Put the nuts or seeds in a dry frying pan over medium heat and toast, stirring almost constantly, until fragrant, 3 to 4 minutes. Larger nuts, such as hazelnuts or almonds, may require more time, 8 to 10 minutes. Transfer immediately to a plate to cool, to avoid burning.

roasting red bell peppers/capsicums

Roasted red bell peppers/capsicums are quite versatile. Use them, for example, in Fettuccini with Spicy Red Pepper and Tomato Sauce (page 112). These soft, sweet vegetables are also excellent as an appetizer on their own, simply drizzled with a little olive oil, then seasoned with salt and freshly ground pepper. They make fine additions to salads and sandwiches, too.

You can buy jarred roasted red peppers, often packed in olive oil or a vinegar-spiked brine. However, they rarely taste as good as the home-roasted version, which is easy to prepare. If you don't plan to use immediately, store them with their skins on, refrigerated, in a plastic container for up to 1 week. Peeled and marinated in olive oil, they will last longer—up to 2 weeks.

5 red bell peppers/capsicums

Preheat the oven to 400°F/200°C/gas 6. Place the bell peppers/capsicums in a large roasting pan/tray or baking dish and place in the oven. Roast until the tops begin to change color from red to black, 20 to 30 minutes. Remove from the oven and let cool.

Pull the vegetables partially apart, use your fingers to rub the seeds away, and peel off the skins. Pull them into quarters or halves for storage.

cooking dried beans

Dried beans are inexpensive and nutritious, and they require only a minimal amount of effort to cook. At its simplest, that effort involves an overnight (or at least 8-hour) water soak to render the beans soft enough for cooking. It's so easy, but many home cooks forget about the soak until too close to dinner time.

Fortunately, a "shortcut" method can reduce preparation time to about 2 hours. Both methods are outlined below.

OVERNIGHT OR 8-HOUR SOAK

2 cups/400 g dried beans   2 tsp salt

Rinse and pick over the beans, removing any pebbles or discolored beans. Place in a large bowl and cover by 2 in/5 cm with cold water. Let the beans soak overnight or for at least 8 hours. Drain the beans, rinse well, and transfer to a large pot. Add fresh water to cover by 2 in/5 cm and bring to a boil over high heat. Add the salt, reduce the heat to medium-low, and cook, uncovered, until tender, 45 minutes to 1 hour. Drain again.

SHORTCUT SOAK

2 cups/400 g dried beans   2 tsp salt

Rinse and pick over the beans, removing any pebbles or discolored beans. In a large pot, combine about 8 cups/2 l water and the salt. Bring to a boil over high heat. Add the beans, cover, and boil for 5 minutes. Remove from the heat and let soak, covered, for 1 to 1½ hours. Drain the beans in a colander and return them to the pot.

Cover with fresh water by 2 in/5 cm and bring to a boil. Reduce the heat to medium-low, simmer, uncovered, until tender, 30 to 45 minutes. Drain again.

scraping a vanilla bean/pod

Grown in tropical climates, vanilla beans/pods are the dried seed pods that enhance flavors in many sweet and savory foods. Vanilla extract/essence can easily substitute for the pod. But when infusing milk with vanilla flavor, it can be argued that the true bean gives a purer flavor. Since a pod is quite simple to prepare for cooking, it's worth the effort to give it a try and see for yourself. Vanilla beans/pods can be found in most specialty-food spice sections.

Lay the vanilla bean/pod flat on a cutting surface. Using a sharp paring knife, slice open lengthwise. Scrape out the pastelike seeds from the interior. You can use the seeds or reserve the bean pod for use in cooking, depending on what is called for in a recipe. More often than not, it is the bean that is saved, but not always (see Pear Clafouti, page 206, and Polenta Cake, page 201).

simple syrup

makes about
1½ cups/
360 ml syrup

There's a reason they call it "simple": It really is. Yet some individuals think a simple syrup is too difficult to make, and they shy away from recipes that include it. This standard syrup is commonly used to sweeten many homemade beverages, and it is used in a number of recipes throughout this book, including the Sparkling Wine Granité (page 182)—actually a frozen beverage—as well as several sparkling Chandon cocktails (page 49). With 5 minutes of prep time and only two ingredients, simple syrup will surely become a foundation item in your drinks repertoire.

1 cup/240 ml water　　　　　　　　　　　**1 cup/200 g sugar**

In a small saucepan, combine the water and sugar and bring to a boil over medium-high heat, stirring occasionally until the sugar has dissolved, 3 to 4 minutes. Remove from the heat and let cool to room temperature. Use immediately, or refrigerate in a glass jar for up to 1 month.

vegetable stock

Vegetable stock can be made from a wide variety of vegetables. The following recipe is a simple standard that can also stand in for chicken stock. It can be used in a variety of recipes in this book. For richer color and flavor, the skins are left on the onions. There is no need to peel the garlic cloves, either.

2 medium yellow onions with skins intact, rinsed, ends trimmed, and quartered

4 celery stalks with leaves, cut into 2-in/5-cm lengths

3 garlic cloves, quartered

10 to 15 fresh flat-leaf (Italian) parsley sprigs

2 bay leaves

2 tsp salt

In a large pot, combine 2 qt/2 l water, the onions, celery, garlic, parsley, bay leaves, and salt. Bring to a boil over high heat. Reduce the heat to low and simmer, uncovered, for 40 minutes, occasionally skimming off any foam that forms on the surface. Remove from the heat and let cool. Strain through a fine-mesh sieve or a colander lined with cheesecloth/muslin; discard the solids. Refrigerate in airtight containers for up to 1 week, or freeze for up to 3 months.

chicken stock

Chicken stock is a remarkably helpful cooking aid. It serves to heighten flavors in dishes where water alone might not be as effective. This is most obvious when cooking something as simple as rice. It is used in numerous recipes throughout this book such as Crab and Corn Bisque with Chervil Oil (page 97) or Foie Gras Risotto (page 116). To make the stock, use leftover chicken and chicken bones from a roast chicken. Or you can also use raw, fresh chicken, which may give you a bit more flavor. Leftover chicken is obviously not only more practical, but also more economical. It's easy to make a little stock each time you roast a chicken. Then store it in the freezer.

When you need chicken stock but have none on hand, canned or boxed commercial chicken broth makes a good substitute. Purchase low-salt (or low-sodium) versions, however, because many commercial broths are salty enough to throw off your recipe measurements.

2 to 3 lb/1 to 1.5 kg cooked chicken carcass or raw chicken parts such as backs, wings, and necks

1 yellow onion, coarsely chopped

1 large carrot, peeled and coarsely chopped

4 garlic cloves

½ tsp dried thyme

1 bay leaf

1 tsp salt

In a large pot, combine 3 qt/3 l water, the chicken, onion, carrot, garlic, thyme, bay leaf, and salt. Bring to a boil over high heat. Reduce the heat to low and simmer, uncovered, for 1½ hours, occasionally skimming off any foam that collects on the surface. Remove from the heat and strain through a fine-mesh sieve or a colander lined with cheesecloth/muslin into a clean container.

Discard the solids and let the stock cool. Cover and refrigerate until the fat congeals on the surface, 2 to 3 hours. Remove and discard the fat. Use the stock immediately, or refrigerate in air-tight containers for up to 3 days. Freeze for up to 3 months.

veal stock and demi-glace

makes about
2 qt/2 l stock
or about
2 cups/480 ml
demi-glace

Like any stock, veal stock makes an excellent addition to soups and sauces. It can easily stand in for chicken stock, but its unusually powerful flavor makes it very effective in intense sauces such as the ones used for Pork Loin Chops with Ricotta Gnocchi in Sage Butter (page 157) and Braised Veal Cheeks with Celery Root Purée (page 168). Veal stock requires a little more effort to make than other stocks, and those individuals who don't have time to make it from scratch will be relieved to note that commercial substitutes are available in most specialty-food shops. Don't be embarrassed about buying your demi-glace, a highly concentrated veal stock described in more detail below. Commercial demi-glace is easy to rehydrate with water and provides a very effective stand-in for veal stock.

To dilute homemade or commercial demi-glace for use as veal stock, mix 1 part demi-glace with about 4 parts hot water. Bring to a gentle simmer over medium-high heat and whisk until fully dissolved. Taste and adjust the proportions as needed; a good stock base should taste fairly rich but not overly so.

4 to 5 lb/2 to 2.5 kg veal bones, cut into 3-in/7.5-cm pieces

2 or 3 veal shanks (about 2 lb/1 kg total weight), cut into 3-in/7.5-cm pieces

½ cup/118 ml tomato paste/tomato purée

1 bottle (750 ml) dry red wine

10 to 15 black peppercorns

2 yellow onions, coarsely chopped

1 carrot, peeled and coarsely chopped

1 celery stalk, coarsely chopped

1 bay leaf

5 qt/4.7 l water

3 to 5 fresh flat-leaf (Italian) parsley sprigs

Preheat the oven to 450°F/230°C/gas 8. Place the bones and shanks in a roasting pan/tray and roast, turning occasionally, until browned on all sides, about 1 hour. Transfer the bones and shanks to a large pot. Add the tomato paste/tomato purée and cook over medium-high heat, stirring frequently, until it turns a dark, reddish brown. Add the wine and stir to scrape up any browned bits from the bottom of the pot. Add the peppercorns, onions, carrot, celery, and bay leaf. Reduce the heat to medium and cook for 10 minutes longer. Add the water, bring to a boil over high heat, and reduce the heat to maintain a simmer. Add the parsley and continue to simmer, uncovered, for about 5 hours, occasionally skimming off any foam that collects on the surface.

Strain through a sieve and let cool. (Discard the solids.) Refrigerate for 3 hours, then discard the fat that congeals on top. Cover and refrigerate for up to 3 days, or freeze for up to 3 months.

TO MAKE DEMI-GLACE: Bring the finished veal stock to a boil and reduce the heat to maintain a simmer. Cook, uncovered, until the stock has reduced to about 2 cups/480 ml of thick brown liquid, about 2 hours. Refrigerate in an airtight container for up to 3 days, or freeze for up to 3 months.

index

Acknowledgments

Writing a book is often a group effort, and this book is a dream that required years of collaboration. It would never have happened without the enthusiasm and support of Domaine Chandon CEO, Malcolm Dunbar. Throughout the entire process, Malcolm's vision, dedication, and friendship kept the project on course. Also on the front lines, Domaine Chandon public relations wizard Lara Abbott was a key figure in managing the daily minutiae that would have driven a lesser mortal insane. Thank you, Lara, for your ongoing courage and assistance.

I would also like to thank Domaine Chandon *chef de cuisine* Perry Hoffman and pastry chef Francisco Enriquez, who created many of the delicious recipes found in these pages. In addition to Perry and Francisco, acknowledgment also goes to all former Domaine Chandon chefs—in particular, Philippe Jeanty, Robert Curry, and Chris Manning.

Domaine Chandon is the only Napa Valley winery with its own restaurant. This has created a uniquely creative relationship between the chefs and the winemakers. As a result, winemaker Tom Tiburzi has been instrumental in recipe development at the restaurant. During the writing of this book, Tom also provided in-depth information about winemaking at Domaine Chandon and generously shared with me his considerable knowledge about wine in general.

Of course, what's a book without a publisher? Chronicle Books editor Bill LeBlond gave me my first opportunity as an author a decade ago. Since then, we have produced many fine books. I am particularly proud of this one and forever grateful for Bill's support. I would like to thank Chronicle's Sara Schneider for her fabulous design work and Sarah Billingsley for her ability to hold the center together. And let's not forget that every good writer needs a great copy editor. For *The Domaine Chandon Cookbook*, I was blessed with Carrie Bradley, whose attention to detail and understanding of both writing and cooking was indispensable.

Speaking of cooking, readers should note that recipes prepared by talented professional chefs in their professional kitchens still require testing in something resembling a home kitchen. It's the only way to be sure that a restaurant's magic can be translated for home cooks as well. My wife, partner, and collaborator, Jodie Morgan, has tested more recipes than most of us could imagine. She does it well, and (almost) always with a smile.

Also working behind the scenes, my agent, Carole Bidnick, played a critical role in the creation of this book. Carole believed in the project from the very beginning. Without her professional acumen, patience, and really good instincts, it's unlikely that I would be writing these acknowledgments today. Thank you, Carole, for all of your efforts.

The artistry that occurs in the restaurant and winery, as well as the natural beauty surrounding Domaine Chandon's Napa Valley estate, cannot be captured in words alone. France Ruffenach has given life to these pages with her magnificent photographs and shared her exceptional vision with all of us. Food stylist George Dolese should also be commended for his work.

Finally, every book needs to be promoted. Heartfelt thanks go to Domaine Chandon's marketing team, led by Ryan Harris and Michael Stedman, as well as Chronicle Books' marketing director Peter Perez and publicist David Hawk.

—Jeff Morgan